The Next Step:

50 MORE THINGS YOU CAN DO TO SAVE THE EARTH

The EarthWorks Group

Andrews and McMeel
A Universal Press Syndicate Company
Kansas City

To Jesse, who hasn't taken his *first* step yet.

THIS BOOK IS PRINTED ON RECYCLED PAPER.

Created and packaged by Javnarama
Designed by Javnarama

ISBN 0-8362-2302-0
First Edition 10 9 8 7 6 5 4 3 2 1

Library of Congress Catalog Card Number: 90-85467

We've provided a great deal of information about
practices and products in our book. In most cases,
we've relied on advice, recommendations and research
by others whose judgments we consider accurate and
free from bias. However, we can't and don't guarantee
the results. This book offers you a start.
The responsibility for using it
ultimately rests with you.

Andrews and McMeel books are available at quantity discounts
with bulk purchase for educational, business or sales promotional use.
For information, please contact:
Andrews and McMeel
4900 Main Street
Kansas City, Missouri 64112

ACKNOWLEDGMENTS

The EarthWorks Group would like to thank everyone who worked with us to make this book possible, including:

- John Javna
- John Dollison
- Nancy Skinner
- Fritz Springmeyer
- Catherine Dee
- Lenna Lebovich
- Fawn Smiley
- Lyn Speakman
- Melanie Foster
- Seth Zuckerman
- Phil Catalfo
- Julie Bennett
- Stuart Schare
- Robin Kipke Alkire
- Nenelle Bunnin
- Patty Glikbarg
- Jack Mingo
- Roger Rappaport
- Gil Friend
- Jay Nitschke
- Andy Sohn
- Recycle America
- Valentine Paredes
- Carolyn Marshall
- Mike Goldberger
- Sherilyn Hovin

- Dayna Macy
- Mike Morey
- Bob Drews
- Debra Lynn Dadd
- George Everett
- Chris Calwell
- Tom Auzenne
- Maggie Gainer
- Tracy Grubbs
- Steve Weissman
- Marydele Donnelly
- Jeremy Sherman
- Daren Fields
- Regina Minudri
- Terri Roberts
- Terry O'Sullivan
- Rich Kuzmyak
- Mark Wright
- Ellen Fletcher
- Tom Murdoch
- Rebecca Mayeno
- Jim Sayer
- Joel Makower
- Jean Gardner
- Barbara Pitschel
- Michael Herz

- James Nixon
- Mel Duncan
- Gene Karpinsky
- Suzanne Head
- Barbara Shapiro
- Diane Sherman
- Ed and Sharon Rugg
- Renee Kivikko
- Julie Stone
- Gary Cohen
- Brett A. Fisher
- Steve Romalewski
- Brian Lipsett
- Jim Jensen
- Sarah Dewey
- Eudora Russell
- Caren Cunico
- Betty Brickson
- Trish Ferrand
- Victoria Fields
- Bob Scowcroft
- Albert Donnay
- Gar Smith
- George Everett
- Rick and Sandy Meyers
- Mike Williamson
- Denise Sobel
- Linda Brown, Green Cross
- Pamela Brown
- Fred Meyer
- Randy Ziglar
- Brenda Mizrahi
- Maureen Mageau-DeCindis
- Marco Kaltofen
- Richard Atkinson
- Dick Mark, 20/20 Vision
- Joe E. Arguello
- Jerry Alexander
- Richard Conlin
- Diana Gale
- Maggie Etheredge
- Michael Carr
- Edith Felchle
- Maurine Lauber
- Robin Doctorman
- Cindy Philips
- Clarence Taylor
- Marianne Hegeman
- Kathleen and Brigid Sullivan
- Carolyn & Jessica Lyman
- Paul J. Godfrey
- Robert Randall
- Karen O'Leary
- Lucinda Muniz Hale
- Chuck Moore
- Brandon King
- Jon Kirby
- The Folks at Bette's To Go
- Beth Weinberger
- Bruce Dickinson
- Paul Downton

CONTENTS

INTRODUCTION

When we published *50 Simple Things You Can Do to Save the Earth* in the fall of 1989, we hoped a few thousand people might find it helpful.

But within months, it was one of the best-selling environmental books in history.

We were astounded. We didn't realize that people were so ready to do something to save the planet.

50 Simple Things was an important first step. Judging from our mail, people now feel they can really do something to improve the environment; there's a new sense that they can make a difference. They've switched to canvas shopping bags, bought low-phosphate detergents, started recycling aluminum cans, and planted trees.

But we're concerned about what happens next. Snipping six-pack rings may be a start, but it's not the solution. It's important to harness that enthusiasm and new-found sense of personal power to take The Next Step. It's time to reach out to the community.

You don't have to be the head of a company to help a business change, and you don't have to be an elected official to help get the government to act. You just need a vision of what you're trying to accomplish, why it's important, and a clear sense of how to do it. That's what you'll find in this book. It isn't a comprehensive guide—it doesn't try to tell you every detail. But the projects are carefully laid out, and there are plenty of resources available to get you started. And the projects aren't theoretical. All of them have been successfully done in neighborhoods around America and Canada.

Don't read this as *50 Things You Should Do*—it's an overview of what's possible. You couldn't do all 50 things if you tried; they're too involved. The important thing is to pick a project that appeals to you, and make a commitment to it. You'll be an inspiration. And you'll be doing all you can to protect the most important resource we have—the Earth.

My son Jesse, who was born about a week after *50 Simple Things Kids Can Do* was published, is now almost a year old. Every day I see joy and hope in his eyes; he has no concept of the dangers we face. For him, and for all the Earth's children, take The Next Step.

—John Javna,
The EarthWorks Group
March 17, 1991

A YEAR LATER...

As we approach Earth Day 1991, the signs of positive change are everywhere. Grocery stores that once contributed to the solid waste crisis are now helping to prevent it. Utilities that once pushed customers to use more energy are now paying the same customers to save it. New magazines, clubs, and businesses dedicated to environmental protection are blooming across the landscape.

You can take credit for this. You're not just buying books—you're using them. You're voting with your dollars and actions for a better world.

• Until last year, the Direct Marketing Association annually received about 90,000 letters from consumers asking to have their names removed from national mailing lists. But in 1990, more than a million people asked the DMA to stop their junk mail.

• In 1987, about 4 million energy-saving compact fluorescent bulbs were sold in the U.S. By 1990, an estimated 14 million were being sold every year...and the figure is still skyrocketing.

• In 1987, 1.3 billion pounds of aluminum cans were collected for recycling. By 1989, Americans were returning 340 million more pounds each year. Nearly 61 percent of all cans sold were recycled, and return rates were on the rise in 1990.

Small actions don't seem so small when millions of people are doing them at the same time. Now imagine how much more we can accomplish if we try something bigger.

Now that we've figured out how to recycle at home, we can enter the local political process to bring curbside recycling to everyone. By steering our dollars toward recycled and efficient products, we can ensure wider availability of the products. By encouraging service organizations to get involved in the environmental movement, we ensure that it has strong local roots.

If 1990 was about making changes in your own life to benefit the Earth, 1991 is about multiplying that action by the efforts of your family, friends, and community. Multiplication is always harder to learn than addition, but it's also faster and more powerful once you get the hang of it.

Taking The Next Step means converting the power of individual action into collective action. We can do it!

—Chris Calwell,
Natural Resources Defense Council
(NRDS), February 19, 1991

WHAT'S

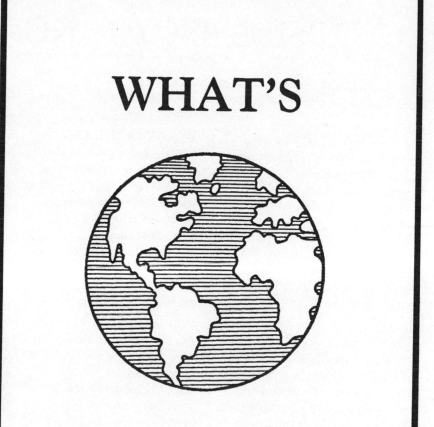

HAPPENING

CURBSIDE RECYCLING

Maggie Etheredge launched a campaign to bring curbside recycling to Elloree, South Carolina, a town of 905 people.

A RECYCLED IDEA

"I was brought up recycling. My little sister and I used to fight over who was going to stomp on the cans to make them flat. In the early '70s, I worked as a volunteer for a recycling program in Columbia, South Carolina. It didn't last. People didn't believe in recycling back then. But now we know better."

TOO MUCH GARBAGE

"I'd seen a need for recycling in Elloree for a long time. I was concerned about cutting down the amount of garbage that was going to our county landfill—in less than five years it will be full. I saw no reason not to start a recycling program!"

HELP WANTED

"I found a couple of people who were interested in helping. They jumped on the idea like a chicken on a june bug. We went and looked at the recycling program in Aiken, South Carolina. I was amazed at how simple it was."

WINNING THEM OVER

"We showed the town council how easy it would be to have curbside recycling By recycling and picking up garbage only once week, the town could save $30,000 a year. But the council still took three months to make up its mind."

PICKING UP SPEED

"We decided to recycle glass, paper, plastic, tin, aluminum, used car batteries, and used oil. I collected grape crates from the local food chain for the curbside bins. Since we already had curbside garbage pick up, all we had to do was put some barrels on a pick up truck and drive a wagon behind it to hold paper."

RECYCLING SENSATION

"We set out to raise awareness about what we're doing to the earth. People were willing to recycle. We went from 'Recycle, Elloree!' to 'Elloree Recycles.' It's heartening to drive around town and see the recycling crates by the garbage bins."

A DIAPER SERVICE

Denise Sobel is a nurse in Novato, California. She persuaded Novato Community Hospital to start using a diaper service.

DIAPERS ARE FOREVER
"About three years ago, I was walking my dog along a dirt road near my house, and I noticed a used disposable diaper along the side of the road. I walk down that road a lot, and I noticed it every day."

...AND EVER
"Well, six months later, the diaper was still there, and hadn't changed a bit. That's when I decided to try to convince my hospital to switch to a diaper service. Meanwhile, the diaper was still there by the side of the road—rain or shine, wind, everything—and stayed there for three years, until a car finally ran it over it and destroyed it. I felt funny leaving it there for three years, but I wanted to see what would happen to it."

DOWN WITH DISPOSABLES
"It took a month or two for the hospital administration to see that I was serious about changing to a diaper service."

PIN THEM DOWN
"Some of the staff wanted to stay with disposables. But I finally convinced them to give it a try. That started the ball rolling."

DIAPER DEAL
"It didn't take us long to realize that the diaper service cost only half as much as disposables cost. We were only paying 10¢ per diaper for the diaper service, compared to 21¢ per diaper for disposables."

HOSPITAL HEADLINES
"Once the word got out that we had made the switch, the local TV station interviewed us, and we started getting phone calls from hospitals all over the west coast asking about it."

CLOTH CAME THROUGH
"Before we started using the diaper service, some of the nurses didn't want to switch. But once the diaper service began, they changed their minds. Nobody wants to go back now. We're totally committed."

Asphalt made with old tires has three times the life span of concrete.

TOXICS CLEAN UP

Dick Mark is the executive director of 20/20 Vision, an organization devoted to organizing grassroots letter writing campaigns. In September 1990, 20/20 Vision led a campaign to divert money from the MX Missile Program into a fund for cleaning up toxic waste at military bases.

DOWN IN THE DUMPS

"Since World War II, the U.S. military has been the nation's top polluter, exempt from the laws that require everyone else to clean up toxic waste sites. The Department of Defense has acknowledged that there are over 14,000 potentially contaminated sites—including air force and army bases, depots—places where they've been dumping waste for years."

THAT'S WRITE

"Two bills were introduced co-operatively to get the military to clean up these sites. We worked with Friends of the Earth to get the word out about the bills. We asked our members in four congressional districts to write to their representatives—four key congressional leaders who were on defense committees or could be influential if they spoke up."

LETTER RIP

"This campaign proved that citizens really can make a difference. The four congressional offices received 200-400 letters each. That made the representatives sit up and take notice—it was obvious there was a groundswell of support for this."

ENVIRONMENTAL LAW

"The four representatives co-sponsored legislation to shift money into the toxic cleanup fund. Members of Congress in other districts also received mail supporting it, so they joined in. There was so much support that the legislation was adopted without a vote—we got $46 million out from the MX Missile Program."

A CLEAN RECORD

"It was dramatic that Congress was willing to take money away from a weapons system and put it into environmental cleanup. We hope it's going to set a precedent."

Oregon continues to lose 10 square miles of ancient forest each month.

A COMMUNITY GARAGE SALE

Marianne Hegeman organized a community garage sale in El Cerrito, California.

A SHAKY START

"Our reason for having a community garage sale was unusual. We had the Loma Prieta earthquake in October 1989, and homeowners needed to have their foundations inspected. But many of the basements of these homes were filled with old belongings and other stuff that had to be removed before inspectors could examine the foundations."

ALL TOGETHER NOW

"That's what gave me the idea to organize a city-wide garage sale: If everyone had a sale on the same day, we would attract a lot of business and sell more stuff. And that way, things wouldn't get thrown away—they'd be reused."

LET'S HALF A SALE

"I went to the city with my idea, and they liked it. They agreed to give a half-price seismic inspection to anyone who particpated in the garage sale."

WHERE IT'S AT

"The city also helped publicize it. We made forms available. Participants filled in their names and addresses, and we published the list, as well as a map showing sale locations."

AD IT UP

"The city printed this up and distributed hundreds of them around town a week before the sale. We also let local TV and radio stations know about the sale. They were helpful in getting the word out."

SALE OF THE CENTURY

"There were more more than 160 individual sales, and people came from all over the area to visit them. High schools had sales, as well as senior citizens communities, and other city groups."

LEFTOVERS AGAIN

"We had a Goodwill dropoff point for things that didn't sell. So all the leftovers went to charities."

Water saving devices can shrink your water flow 30,000 gallons a year.

GREEN LABELING

Pamela Brown is assistant vice president for Fred Meyer Stores in Portland, Oregon—one of the first retail stores to label "green" products for consumers

PEOPLE POWER
"Our company has over 22,000 employees. We're consumers; we're all aware of environmental issues. We look at what we buy and see what could be improved."

READ THE LABEL
"Some of us came together and said, 'Here's something we can do in our workplace.' We started reading product labels, asking questions about products, calling the 800 numbers. We asked the same questions everyone else would: 'Is it recyclable? Reusable? Good for the Earth?' We came out with our own in-house labeling system based on this research."

CERTIFIED GREEN
"But we're not scientists. There was a national independent certification program called Green Cross starting up. We switched to their program since it was based on scientific testing."

THE WORD IS OUT
"In the seven states where we have stores, people sit up and take notice of what we've done. Having this program has definitely increased environmental awareness in our area. For example, in Snohomish County, Washington, we gave the solid waste management department 2,000 brochures to distribute locally."

ACROSS THE USA
"It's inspired a lot of other people, too. They've called us from about 30 different places: Florida, Alaska, Tennessee, Wisconsin...members of the Dutch government have even come to see me. Their question is always the same: 'How did you do that?'"

CONSUMERS COUNT
"Educating consumers really does help change their buying habits. People want to buy products that are good for the Earth. And they vote every day with their pocketbooks."

Making a standard disposable battery uses 50 times more power than it generates.

ADOPTING A STREAM

Brandon King is a fifth-grade teacher at Jackson Elementary School in Everett, Washington. In 1983, he helped the school "adopt" a local stream.

UP A CREEK

"We knew Pigeon Creek was in trouble. It used to be said that it 'ran red with salmon,' but 20 years ago, it began dying. And by 1983, the salmon were completely gone."

WISH GRANTED

"We applied to the county government for a $1,300 grant to adopt the stream. We got the grant and bought a 55-gallon aquarium to start raising salmon."

A NEW DAY SPAWNING

"We bought 1,000 salmon eggs from a state hatchery and put them in the aquarium. We also started monitoring the water quality of the creek. We check for dissolved oxygen, nitrogen, pH, etc. on a regular basis."

IN THE SWIM

"We taught the kids that adopting the stream meant they had to take on the responsibilities of adoptive parents—they had to take care of the salmon babies and keep the creek clean."

SCHOOL OF FISH

"In October, the kids pick litter out of the stream. In November, when the salmon return to the creek, the school has a 'Salmon Celebration.' In May, when the aquarium fish are old enough, the kids release them into the stream."

WRITE ON TARGET

"In addition to organizing the students to save Pigeon Creek, the school staff has formed a group called Streamkeepers that's involved in letter writing campaigns and other projects."

DAM IF YOU DO

"Last year, the city of Everett began building a $700,000 storm water retention facility, which will help improve the water quality of the creek. The facility had been delayed for a number of years. The activities of Jackson Elementary were important in finally getting the project off the ground."

Every day, 3,500 acres of rural America are bulldozed for buildings and highways.

A BIKE-FRIENDLY CITY

Michael "the 2-Wheeled" Carr has been working to make roads safer for bicyclists in Dallas, Texas since 1983. He's a board member of the Greater Dallas Bicyclists.

STRESSED OUT

"I started running to reduce stress from my job. My body told me I couldn't handle it, so I switched to bicycling. But I found out fast that bicyclists are treated like second class citizens. Once a driver turned left in front of me, I hit the car's trunk, flipped over and rolled alongside the shoulder. The police officer asked me where I worked, and since I was between contracts, I said I wasn't working. He said, 'It figures.'"

WHERE THERE'S A WHEEL...

"It started to become clear to me that bicycle riders are discriminated against by people like police officers and engineers who design roads. As bicycling became part of my life, I realized nobody was looking out for the needs of bicyclists."

BEATING THE SYSTEM

"So I got things started. Now in Dallas, bicycle advocates have created a system of bike routes that allows you to ride from one part of town to another without getting on major roads very much. You do have to get on major roads to cross freeways, rivers and railroad tracks. In those areas, we're encouraging the city to pave wide outside lanes."

THE GREEN LIGHT

"Traffic signals have now been adjusted so they'll turn green when there's only a bicyclist waiting. Police harrassment has practically disappeared, and a $12 million dollar bridge with wide outside lanes was built over the Trinity River."

ON A ROLL

"Here's my advice for people who want to make their town bicycle friendly: It helps to form an organization. You want the government to think of your group as a herd of aroused, concerned citizens. Keep track of people, get them involved, have them speak out regularly—and your group will appear to be ten times larger than it is."

Five recycled PET bottles make enough fiberfill to stuff a ski jacket.

COMPOSTING

Randy Ziglar is one of 200 gardeners who have plots at Ocean View Farms, the largest community garden in Los Angeles. He's helped the gardeners start a community composting project.

WORTHY WEEDS

"A lot of gardeners used to throw away extra plants and weeds. We'd fill up four trash bins a week. Then we realized that trash costs were our greatest expense. We suddenly became more interested in our expensive trash, and we discovered that it contained at least 50% material we grew in the garden."

IT'S ONLY NATURAL

"A few gardeners began to ask, 'Why not compost it?' It seemed like a good idea—creating something really wonderful, which is compost that feeds the soil and nurtures plants—and eliminating something really terrible, which is pollution."

WHEEL OF PROGRESS

"We wanted to cut our waste costs 50%. We put up signs asking gardeners to take weeds and shrubs to the compost area. The gardeners learned to put their garden materials in a wheelbarrow and take it to the orchard."

IT'LL TURN UP

"Every Saturday, volunteers make and turn the compost piles. The finished compost gets used up real quick. The problem is not in using it, but in having enough for everybody."

THE PLOT THICKENS

"Three years ago, I'd say less than 5% of the gardeners composted. Now, I'd say 25-50% of them actually make compost on their own plots."

A LIGHTER LOAD

"We reduced our normal four bins of trash to two. So we cut our waste disposal costs in half—from $2,400 to $1,200 a year."

FERTILE GROUNDS

"Now that we have compost, many of the gardeners don't have to buy fertilizer. We've become more self sufficient, self reliant; instead of depending on a commercial cycle, we depend on community networking."

Some paper can be recycled 7 times or more.

SAVING RAINFORESTS

Jon Kirby is a teacher at Erindale Secondary School in Mississauga, Ontario, Canada. He started a student environmental club and helped the members make money to save the rainforests.

NO CLASS
"I felt there was no vehicle for environmental action at school. The curriculum was improving, but environmental studies were rarely discussed in class."

FOR THE FOREST
"After we started the club, the kids planned a two week-long series of events to teach the school about the rainforest and the problems it faces, and raise money to help save it."

FOR THE EFFECT
"We made up a questionnaire— a multiple choice survey that was passed out to every student. The purpose was to gauge the impact the students and their families were having on the rainforest. The club collected the information and analyzed the results to show people how to change their habits."

GREEN ACRES
"Each homeroom was asked to raise $25 to buy one acre of rainforest land—and they were encouraged to be creative."

TAKING AIM
"One class had a dart board booth—for $1, students could throw darts at pictures of members of a controversial rock group. Some students even bought rainforest acres for their families for Christmas. By the end of the week every class had met or exceeded its goal."

A PIE FOR AN EYE...
"Teachers also provided their own incentives for raising money. Some teachers matched the money their students raised dollar for dollar. The vice principals held a raffle, and the winners got to throw pies in their faces."

NEW GROWTH
"The kids raised $7,000 to save the rainforest. But the success went deeper—the kids proved to themselves that they could make a difference if they set their minds to it, and that's one of the most important things they can learn at their age."

An energy-efficient appliance can use as much as 50% less energy than a regular one.

A GARDEN

Clarence Taylor manages the Cashmere Community Garden in Houston, Texas. He works with an organization called Target Hunger and donates some of the vegetables he grows to local food pantries.

HUNGER PANGS

"I used to see people getting food out of those garbage dumpsters behind supermarkets. Many times, I'd just give them five or ten dollars, but that wasn't really solving the problem."

FOOD FOR THOUGHT

"There were three reasons I wanted to have a community garden. I felt I could help by providing fresh vegetables. I thought it would be good if we could grow vegetables without using so many chemicals. And I hoped people would want to get involved."

SEEING IS BELIEVING

"Before I started, I went to another garden to find out how to set it up. I saw that we could grow all types of vegetables— we'd be putting a vacant lot to good use and beautifying the city."

IT HELPS A LOT

"Most people with vacant lots will let you use them because they're tired of paying so much money to get rid of the weeds and cut the grass. One of my friends referred me to a woman who owns a lot. She said I could do whatever I wanted with the space."

PUT IT TO BED

"Most of the land is dry and you can't work it. So we made raised beds—we took newspapers and put them on the grass four or five sheets thick. Then we put soil on top of the paper. It's less work that way."

LAY IT ON THE TABLE

"The garden produces about 18,000 pounds of vegetables in the spring, and about 15-16,000 pounds in the fall. Each day, five other people and I go out and pick okra, tomatoes, greens, beans, potatoes, onions, lettuce, carrots, beets…you name it. We give nine food pantries fresh vegetables about once a week."

Mowing the lawn for half an hour can produce as much smog as driving a new car 172 miles.

ORGANIC SHOPPING

Brenda Mizrahi and her friends convinced their local grocer to stock organic produce at his store in Malibu, California.

NO MORE PESTICIDES

"I knew three other people who were concerned about toxic chemicals on our food. We're all mothers, and we were especially concerned about our children. Not that we weren't concerned about ourselves, but when you have kids, it's a different story."

CITIZEN COALITION

"Right after the Alar scare, we formed a group called Action For Safe Food. It started as a health issue, but we eventually became concerned about the environment and the whole picture."

SMART SHOPPING

"We asked the owner of Alexander's Market to consider getting organically grown produce because there was a market for it. We pointed out that he could attract a lot of new business this way."

ORGANIC PANIC

"The owner was defensive at first. The thing about organics is you can't have whatever you want any time of year—organic foods are what's in season. That was one of his concerns. And he didn't want to sell organic produce if the prices were going to be so high that it would just sit there."

FARM FACTS

"But he realized he could have both organic and non-organic produce. It basically costs the same for farmers to produce organic or non-organic produce— without chemicals, you can afford more labor. The owner found suppliers that didn't overcharge him, and he treated the organic produce like the rest. So the prices are much lower than they are at health food stores."

A NATURAL

"The people working at the market are excited. And the store has new customers who've never shopped there before!"

Americans throw away enough disposable diapers to fill a barge every 6 hours.

A BUTTERFLY GARDEN

Rebecca Mayeno is a third grade teacher at Jefferson School in Berkeley, California. She started a butterfly garden at the school in 1985.

CLIP & SAVE

"My student teacher brought in a two-sentence clipping from a teaching magazine about butterfly gardens. I thought it sounded like a good idea—a project that offered everything for the kids…plants, animals, digging, pruning, cutting, watching seeds grow…all kinds of things."

WHAT COMES NATURAL

"We went to a local nursery and noticed what plants were actually attracting butterflies. Some lists of 'butterfly-friendly' plants said to buy Lantana, so we looked to see what color Lantana actually had butterflies on it. And we walked around the neighborhood to see what butterflies were in the general area, and what plants they seemed attracted to."

FLYING HIGH

"We got plants that were supposed to attract the adult butterflies. We got instant results. They flocked to them."

SAFE & SOUND

"Over several years, we've only had one case of vandalism. Given the fact that it's a public playground, where there is lots of graffiti and other kinds of minor vandalism, that's remarkable."

MADE IN THE SHADE

"Now we're developing a shade section to the garden. With the help of parents and volunteers, we're building planter boxes and raised flower beds and benches for the kids to sit on."

BUTTERFLY SURPRISE

"We bought some plants called Echium Wildpretii—they're known as 'Towers of Jewels'—that were about 4 inches tall. In a year, they were literally 6-foot high towers! We started with these little twiggy leaves, and all of a sudden we had this *thing*! People asked,'What is it? It's covered with butterflies!'"

As many as 46,000 pieces of plastic have been found per square mile of ocean.

CFC RECYCLING

In 1990, Joe Arguello started a business recycling air conditioning coolant. He services about 30 body shops around Denver and Boulder, Colorado.

SETTING IT FREON

"I've been an auto body repairman for 20 years. Nobody's ever worried about CFCs (Chlorofluorocarbons). We'd just let the freon gas evaporate and replace the refrigerant afterwards. One day, I was working on an air conditioner. As usual, I just opened it up and let the gas out. A mechanic standing next to me pointed out that venting CFCs would soon be illegal."

ARMCHAIR REVELATIONS

"A while later, I was being a couch potato, watching a documentary on the ozone layer. I got to thinking about how there's a market for CFCs to be recycled. A lot of the body shops can't afford or don't want to buy the equipment. I figured I could make it easy for them."

I'LL BUY THAT

"I looked for a vampire unit—the machine that traps and recycles CFCs. I had a hard time finding one—everybody had brochures, but nobody had a unit. Finally a company came out with one. I bought it at a big chain auto parts store for about $3,000. Next thing I know, I'm driving around trying to sell a new idea!"

FRESH AIR

"An auto body repair shop calls me when they have a car with an air conditioner that needs servicing. I go to the shop, take the freon out of the car, and recycle it through my equipment. They do their repairs, then I go back and recharge the air conditioner. I believe in the recycling enough that I don't charge them for that part of my service— I just recycle the coolant and sell it back to them."

THE RIGHT THING TO DO

"Everybody I do work for is delighted. The body shop owners are glad to have this option, to be staying within the laws, even though the laws aren't very well enforced right now."

NO PESTICIDES

Lucinda Muniz Hale lives in Eugene, Oregon. In 1983, she successfully convinced her condominium homeowner's board to stop using pesticides on the condominium grounds.

GROWING NOWHERE
"Most of our decorative plants, and many individually owned plants, such as hanging fuchsias, had been killed by indiscriminate spraying of pesticides. I prepared a handout and distributed copies of the labels from the pesticides that were being used on our grounds."

NEW IDEAS
"I got involved with the Homeowner's Board and headed a committee to rewrite the bid specifications for ground maintenance. I scoured the community looking for non-chemical landscapers. I presented bids to the board—and the board chose a landscaper with a non-chemical background."

FOR THE BIRDS
"Our grounds are now beautifully maintained. They look better than ever, and the birds are back—they had disappeared when the pesticides were being used."

GETTING THE BUGS OUT
"Since then, it's been an ongoing educational campaign, but it's paid off. Every year, the board considers new bids for landscape maintenance, and there's the possibility that a company that uses pesticides will be chosen. But as people become more aware of the problems with chemicals, the education process is becoming a little less difficult."

ANOTHER VICTORY
"In 1985, we had carpenter ants. The immediate response of the board was to get someone to come out and apply chemicals. I had a dickens of a time trying to find somebody else. I finally found an entomologist who wanted to start a chemical free pest control business. We got him to treat our complex without using toxic chemicals. It helped him to develop a methodology and start his business. We helped create a market... Now he has more business than he can handle!"

americans throw away enough disposable plates and cups to give the world a picnic 6 times a year.

A RECYCLING MAP

Marianne Hegeman created a "Recycle and Reuse Map"
for the city of Albany, California.

BRIGHT IDEAS
"I'm a graduate student in the Geography Department at San Francisco State, and one of my courses, a land use seminar, required a class project. So I thought up the idea of making a recycling map."

TREASURE MAP
"The map lists all of the recycling facilities in the area, but it does more than that; it lists all of the shops that buy and sell used items as well. Recycling is about more than just sorting your garbage—it's about reusing things that still have life in them."

IF YOU COULD SEE THEM NOW...
"People want to know visually where stores are located, and also what they sell. They never know where good secondhand stores or recycling centers are; addresses are not enough. People are more likely to use a map than a list of addresses. "

AROUND TOWN
"You need to do a lot of footwork to get this kind of information. So I went around to the stores in the community. I found out which stores buy and sell used goods, and which specialize in specific items, like old books. I included any store or facility that dealt with recycling or reuse."

X MARKS THE SPOT
"I plotted each of these stores on the map. At the bottom of the page, I described what they sell."

IN THE NEWS
"I gave the map to the Albany city officials. They loved it. They took it to a graphic artist and had 5,000 copies printed using money from a grant they'd gotten to promote their recycling program. They used the map as an insert in the city's quarterly newsletter that they mail to Albany residents. They also posted maps in local stores. The maps are popular; after only a year, they had to do another printing."

Alabama recycled 6 millon gallons of motor oil in 1988.

TREE RECYCLING

Chuck Moore led an effort to help form sand dunes by securing old Christmas trees down on a local beach near Pearland, Texas.

SHORING IT UP

"I founded a group within our 4H club called the Sea and Shore Group. We got a call from Charles Moss of the Soil Conservation Service of Texas A&M University. He asked us if we were interested in working on a project to restore the sand dunes that the larger storms often wash away."

SAND TRAP

"His idea was to take old Christmas trees and stake them down onto the beach to trap sand in order to form sand dunes. By restoring the dunes, we hoped to prevent the erosion that was blocking the river."

BLOWIN' IN THE WIND

"As the wind blows through the trees, it deposits sand in them. In 45-60 days, you'll have about two feet of dune. At this point, you have mini-dunes."

GRASS ROOTS SUCCESS

"The next step was to plant saltwater grasses in the mini dunes—these grasses help trap sand, and as their roots grow into the sand, the dune becomes more resistant to storms."

GETTING THE JOB DUNE

"The kids love it. And the community is behind it because it helps minimize flooding during large storms. We figure that during one storm last year the dunes delayed the flooding for 45 minutes. That gives the people who live nearby a lot more time to evacuate."

PICKING UP

"Last year in Texas, there were more than 10,000 trees used on 'Dunes Day.' Most of the communities near the beaches in Texas participate. And a lot of communities support us by having special tree pick up days after Christmas."

In 1989, Americans used 80 billion aluminum cans—and recycled a record 60% of them.

A GREEN PTA

Sharon Rugg is PTA president at Davis Elementary in Marietta, Georgia. She's helped make environmental issues a priority for schools in her area.

BACK TO BASICS

"I was interested in bringing environmental issues to school—I feel that in this day and age with video and computer games, kids are losing touch with the earth. They've got to get reunited with it before they can learn to protect it."

IN THE BEGINNING

"They asked me to be the environmental chair on the PTA board in 1987. I said, 'Sure, what do I do?' They didn't really know. So I spent the first year learning what I could do."

MAKING THE GRADE

"At each grade level, teachers choose a project that students can study all year long, something that gives them a hands-on learning experience. For example, the fourth graders are learning about composting, and the second graders are creating a butterfly garden."

HAVING FUNDS

"We've generated more than $3,000 from school recycling projects in the last two years. We reinvest the money in environmental programs—having guest speakers, doing endangered species 'adoptions,' and developing a wildlife habitat on the school grounds."

MAKING A DIFFERENCE

"When I first got involved, the kids weren't into recycling because the people thought it might be messy. It's amazing how the kids have taken to recycling. And it's exciting to see how they've made an impact on their parents and families at home."

HIGH HOPES

"Now there is a push at a lot of local schools. Our hope is that all the schools in the PTA council, state and country can do it!"

Since 1950, energy consumption in the U.S. has climbed 60%.

FOR

YOURSELF

1. BUYER BE WARY

*The number of products being promoted as
"ecologically sound" tripled from 1990 to 1991.*

BACKGROUND. Confused by the new "eco-speak" on
product labels? Just what are "environmentally friendly" aerosols and "eco-safe" toilet bowl cleaners, anyway?

Don't worry—you don't have to be a rocket scientist to learn
which products are really good for the environment...and which
ones only claim to be. All it takes is a little homework.

DID YOU KNOW

• In a recent U.S. survey, almost 50% of the people questioned
said they didn't believe *any* environmental claims manufacturers
make about their products.

• The government has been slow to protect consumer interests. In
1990 several states passed laws prohibiting false environmental
claims, but the majority of states—as well as the federal government—haven't done anything yet.

• Many products don't live up to their environmental claims. For
example: Aerosols are sometimes labelled "ozone friendly." Apparently that means there are no ozone-depleting CFCs used. But
some of them still contain methyl chloroform, which also damages
the ozone layer.

WHAT YOU CAN DO

• Make an effort to understand the environmental issues that are
being addressed. It's not possible to make an intelligent choice unless you understand how products relate to the problems. Take advantage of the numerous consumer-oriented environmental books
and magazines that are now available.

• See what environmental claims are being made. Check out
stores, ads, etc.

• If you find a product that's making misleading claims, tell people
about it. Complain to the store where you bought the product. If

In the 1989 National Beach Clean-up, 170,805 plastic eating utensils were picked up.

you know of a better supplier, pass this info on to the owner or purchasing agent, and let them know you're also telling your neighbors.

• Be sure to share news of good products.

• Complain to the manufacturer. This works—even with companies as large as Mobil Oil. They agreed to stop promoting their corn starch-based Hefty Trash bags as "degradable" after they ignited a firestorm of public resentment, and were threatened with legal action for misleading advertising by several states.

SOME ECO-TERMS

• **Recyclable** means the product *could* be recycled in the future—it doesn't mean it's recycled. Read carefully; people often get the two terms confused. And even if a product says "recyclable," there isn't necessarily anyplace to recycle it in your area. So it may still have to be thrown away.

• **"Degradable" plastics are essentially a fraud.** Even if they eventually do "break down," they only break down into tinier pieces—leaching toxic chemicals and harming animals that eat the plastic.

• **"Environmentally 'Safe' or 'Environmentally Friendly'."** These phrases are legally meaningless. They're the environmental equivalent of "Have a nice day."

• **All-natural.** Natural doesn't necessarily mean "good for you." Arsenic is all-natural.

RESOURCES

• **The Green Consumer Letter.** Tilden Press, 1526 Conn. Ave. NW, Washington, DC 20036. *Excellent monthly newsletter on the latest consumer info. $27 a year.*

• **The EarthWise Consumer,** PO Box 275, Forest Knolls , CA 94933. (415) 488-4614. *Newsletter published 8 times a year. $20.*

Hi, Mom.

2. A CREDIT TO THE ENVIRONMENT

*On an average day, Americans charge more than
$1.5 billion on their credit cards.*

BACKGROUND. Consumerism certainly isn't the way to save the earth. The more goods we produce, the more strain we put on the planet.

But let's be realistic; we all buy things—and a lot of us do it with credit cards.

So why not turn your credit card into "environmentally sound" plastic? Apply for a card that gives money to an environmental organization. Then you'll be making a donation every time you say "charge it."

CHARGE POWER

• The Environmental Defense Fund, the Sierra Club, the Audubon Society, and about 75 other environmental groups have arranged with banks to sponsor credit cards. They're called "affinity" cards.

• Every time you make a purchase, the bank that sponsors the "affinity" card makes a contribution to the sponsoring group.

• Environmental groups may receive about 5¢ for every $10 purchase you charge on your card. That doesn't sound like much, but it adds up. In 1990, EDF's Nature Card earned them about $125,000.

• Americans make more than $550 billion dollars of credit card purchases every year. If only 1% of these were made with environmental credit cards, environmental groups would receive more than $27,000,000.

HOW AFFINITY CARDS WORK

Let's say you buy something from a store with a VISA or Master-Card; here's what happens:

1. The store automatically pays 2%-3% of your purchase to its bank

About 60% of a disposable diaper is made from wood pulp.

as a processing fee.

2. The store's bank keeps a small part of that 2%-3%, and gives the rest to your bank for having issued the card in the first place.

3. Your bank receives this money in addition to the interest and service charges you're already paying. So it can afford to use some of it for promotional purposes. And that's where the "donation" comes from.

Why would a bank give money away?

It's a "volume discount." Banks figure if you're a member of the Sierra Club, for instance, you'll use the Sierra Club card frequently—and generate more income for them. So they're willing to give as much as .05% of your total bill to the sponsoring group.

SHOP AROUND

• Find an organization that sponsors a card. Check the terms, interest rate and fees.

• How much money is donated for each purchase? The organization either gets a percentage of the amount you charge, or a flat sum per purchase. Note: Some cards pay a group money when you're issued the credit card, others donate a portion of the annual fee, and some do both.

• If you're not into credit cards, look into "message checks" sponsored by groups like Greenpeace. You can use them with any bank.

FOR MORE INFORMATION

• **Message! Check Corp.**, 911 East Pike, PO Box 3206-GB, Seattle, WA, 98114. *Write for an order form. They have a selection of checks from a number of environmental organizations.*

• **VISA Corporate Relations**, PO Box 8999, San Francisco, CA 94128, Attn: Environmental Affinity Card List. *Send for a list of over 50 ecology/ animal protection groups that have VISA cards. Include a SASE.*

• **MasterCard International**, Attn: Stephen Drees, 888 7th Ave., 22nd floor, N.Y.C., NY 10106. *Send for their list of environmental affinity cards. Include a SASE.*

On an average day, Americans make over 43 million credit card purchases.

3. KEEP SCORE

In 1990, 53 bills with the word environment in the title, and 1,169 bills with a reference to the environment somewhere in the text were introduced in Congress.

BACKGROUND. Politicians make a lot of promises at election time. But how many of us really pay attention to what they're doing after they take office? Here is a way to do it: Send for an "environmental scorecard."

JUST THE FACTS
• Some elected officials try to cover up their poor environmental track records. That's called greenscam, and it's getting more common all over the country. For example: In 1990 one senator claimed in campaign commercials that he was "tough on toxic waste." But according to the League of Conservation Voters, "in all the crucial toxic waste votes, he has taken the anti-environmental stance."
• In a radio ad, a senator with a 0% score from the League of Conservation Voters claimed to have been commended by the National Wildlife Federation. The ad was refuted and he was defeated.

WHAT YOU CAN DO
• Send for the League of Conservation Voters' environmental scorecard. They've been publishing it since 1970. It lists how all U.S. Senators and members of the House of Representatives voted on key environmental votes.
• What about local elections? That's tougher. Try the local chapter of the League of Conservation Voters. If there isn't one, try the League of Women Voters, a Sierra Club chapter, or a local environmental group.

SOURCES
The League of Conservation Voters, 1707 L St. NW, Suite 550, Washington, D.C. 20036. (202) 785-VOTE. *A $25 membership includes a free scorecard. The scorecard alone is $5.*

Each Congressional office receives an average of 2,000-5,000 letters...a week!

4. OPERATORS ARE STANDING BY...

Dial 1-800 now...It's free!

BACKGROUND. Is there any way you can tell a large company what you think about its overpackaging or other environmental practices...right now? There may be. Look closely at the package—is there a customer service, toll-free "800" number? That's a direct line to America's largest manufacturers. They want to hear what you have to say.

Use 800 numbers to encourage manufacturers to reduce excess packaging and find alternatives to disposables.

WASTE NOT...

• Americans throw out twice as much packaging as they did in 1960—currently as much as 30% of municipal solid waste is made up of packaging and containers. And experts predict that the amount of plastic packaging we throw away may double in 10 years.

• They listen: Due to consumer complaints, in 1990 Campbell's Soup dropped their Souper Combo, a microwaveable soup and sandwich product with multiple layers of paper and plastic packaging.

WHAT YOU CAN DO

• Call a corporate giant today. If there's no 800 number listed on the product, you can call 800 directory information: 1 (800) 555-1212.

RESOURCES

• **"Consumer's Resource Handbook,"** Consumer Information Center, Pueblo, Colorado 81009 (719)948-3334. *A consumer "how-to" on writing complaint letters, corporate contacts, other info. Free.*

• **Waste Lines,** Environmental Action Foundation, 1525 New Hampshire Ave. NW, Washington, DC 20036. *$10 for a one-year subscription.*

Americans throw away an estimated 440 lbs. of packaging per person annually.

5. THE WRITE STUFF

The U.S. Senate received 48 million pieces of mail in 1989.

B ACKGROUND. You pick up a newspaper in the morning, and there's another story about water pollution. That's it, you've had enough—you're going to write to your congressman and demand that the government take action.

But by the time you've found everything you need—stamps, paper, envelope, address—you're already late for work.

Here's a better solution: Create a letter-writing kit that's always around when you need it.

THE POWER OF LETTERS

• Consumer letters —many from children—played a large part in getting McDonald's to phase out foam containers. They also persuaded Starkist Tuna to become "dolphin-safe."

• Proof that letters count: In Massachusetts, 400 citizens wrote their U.S. Representative about an allocation in the Pentagon budget. The item under consideration: environmentally damaging radio towers. As a result, the congressman took a closer look at the budget request and decided he agreed...and introduced amendments that eliminated $100 million of funding for the towers.

• The rule of thumb many congressmen use is: each letter represents the views of *at least* 100 voters in their district.

WHAT YOU CAN DO

• **Put your letter-writing kit together.** Include a file of addresses. Organize them by category—elected officials, newspapers, corporations, etc.

• Blank postcards are good to have on hand—they're simple to use and just as effective as letters.

• Keep it handy. Put it where you watch television or read the paper—that's probably where you'll use it.

About 15% of energy used to heat your home goes to warming air that leaks in through cracks.

LETTER-WRITING TIPS

• Write about one topic at a time. In your first sentence, state that you oppose or support a bill or issue; legislators often use letters to count the number of people who support or oppose bills.

• If you're writing to a legislator about a bill, make sure you have the right number and title (there are thousands of bills every year). You can find this information by calling your local congressional office.

• If it's appropriate, send a thank you letter once the issue is decided. According to one expert, for every 100-250 letters that legislators receive a week, only about two are thank you letters. If you send a thank you, they may remember you the next time you write.

• "Encourage your kids to write letters, too," a staff person at Senator Albert Gore's office suggests. "It's a great way for them to get involved."

• The best time to write letters to elected officials is when a decision is pending, or when they're about to vote on a particular piece of legislation.

RESOURCES

• **Join 20/20 Vision.** 69 South Pleasant St., #203, Amherst, MA 01002 for info, or call (800) 347-2767. *The name stands for 20 minutes a month (how long it takes to write a letter), and $20 a year (the suggested subscription fee). They'll send you an "action alert" postcard each month outlining a suggested issue or bill to write about...and later, updates on the results of their letter-writing campaigns.*

• **For info on important environmental bills when Congress is in session:** call one of these Washington hotlines: The Sierra Club Hotline: (202) 547-5550; The Audubon Society: (202) 547-9017.

• **Don't have time to write?** You can still make a statement. *Earth-Cards*, by the Write for Action Group. Conari Press, 1339 61st St., Emeryville, CA 94608, $6.95. (415) 596-4040. *Contains pre-written and pre-addressed postcards urging legislators and company officials to take action. There's room on each card for a personal note.*

America loses about 300,000 to 400,000 acres of wetlands every year.

6. IT'S BIN IN YOUR KITCHEN

Americans use an average of 1.5 billion aluminum cans every week.

BACKGROUND. Tired of tripping over those soda cans in your hallway? Sick of staring at your "Leaning tower of Newspapers"? There's a simple solution: Get organized. With just a little effort, you can turn your kitchen into an efficient recycling center.

FIND A PLACE TO PUT THEM

• There's no one perfect place to store recyclables. It depends on your home and recycling habits. Just be sure the spot you pick is convenient. If recycling is inconvenient, you're less likely to stick with it.

• If space is really tight, limit your recycling. Think about recycling just cans or paper. Do what works.

STORAGE TIPS

• One good place to keep recyclables: Under the kitchen sink— especially if that's where the wastebasket is. By changing your aim a little, you can recycle instead of throwing away.

• No room under the sink? A nearby porch or broom closet works.

• Newspapers can be stacked almost anywhere. A cardboard box in the corner of a room or garage will do just fine.

• Recycling more than one item? Remember: You don't have to keep all the recyclables in the same place.

KEEP IT CLEAN

• Some people don't recycle at home because they think it's messy. But it doesn't have to be. The best way to keep things clean is to keep recyclables from stacking up. How? Collect only a day's or

N. Y. City has already used 30,000 tons of recycled glass to make "glassphalt" to pave roads.

week's worth somewhere out of sight (under your sink or in a closet), then transfer items to a larger container outside or in a garage. Afraid used jars or cans will attract pests? Just rinse them when you do the dishes, or run them through the dishwasher when you do your regular load.

BINS, BOXES, BAGS

Now that you have a place to store your recyclables, you need something to put them in.

• **If you have a curbside program**, you can probably use the containers they supply. If you don't, use whatever makes recycling easiest for you.

• **Brown paper bags** are good for crushed cans, plastic bottles, and "mixed" paper. Shopping bags with handles are easiest.

• **Cardboard boxes** are ideal. If you want to get your kids involved, ask them to decorate the boxes. Note: liquor boxes are generally the sturdiest. You can cut in your own handles.

• **Plastic buckets** work well.

• **Stackable plastic recycling bins** allow you to sort and store different kinds of recyclables at the same time. They also save space. Bonus: They're often made of recycled plastic. If you can't find them in a local store, many catalogs sell them.

• **Canvas or woven plastic bags** can be hung on hooks in a closet. One for each item. The drawback: Watch out for drips.

• **Interested in new kitchen furniture?** Recycling cabinets are available.

SIZE COUNTS

• Whatever container you choose, make sure it's a manageable size. If you have to walk down a flight of steps to your car, you don't want to have to carry a container that's too awkward or heavy.

• Speaking of your car, how big is its trunk? That may sound silly, but you need containers that'll fit into your car and lift out easily.

RESOURCES

The Recycler's Handbook, by the EarthWorks Group. Published by EarthWorks Press, 1400 Shattuck Ave., #25, Berkeley, CA 94709. $5.95 postpaid, or check with your local bookstore.

You can produce over 1,000 cherry tomatoes in 4 square feet of land.

7. PLANT A BUTTERFLY GARDEN

There are between 700-750 species of butterflies in North America.

BACKGROUND. If you want to do something to save an endangered species, why not start in your own backyard—with a butterfly garden? Butterflies are an environmental barometer—they're very sensitive to ecological changes. When they're in trouble, so are we.

And butterflies are disappearing—"an indicator," says one butterfly expert,"that we're losing our native landscape and the species it supports." But you can help increase butterfly population by planting a butterfly garden and restoring the plants they need to survive.

DID YOU KNOW

• Butterflies are like hummingbirds—they have a high metabolism and they eat a lot of food. So toxics like pesticides build up in their bodies very quickly and can ultimately kill them. Your garden will give them a pesticide-free source of food and shelter.

• If you plant sweet-scented, colorful flowers in your yard, you already have the beginnings of a butterfly garden—butterflies love them. Depending on where you live, if you plant a willow or a maple tree, you might attract tiger swallowtail butterflies to your yard. Plant a cherry or an apple tree and you might attract white admirals.

• Butterflies are some of nature's most effective pollinators. Like other insects, they transport pollen from plant to plant.

• Every year, hundreds of millions of Monarch butterflies migrate form the Rocky Mountains to the California coast and back again. It takes three or four generations of butterflies to make the entire trip. But according to the Audubon Society, this migration is threatened by deforestation in Mexico and land development in California.

More than half the working population of the U.S. lives within biking range (5 miles) of work

• One hundred years ago, the Xerces butterfly lived in the sand dunes in and around San Francisco. But development wiped the dunes out...and the butterflies became extinct—the first butterfly wiped out by man.

WHAT YOU CAN DO

• **Become a butterfly expert.** Find out from a local naturalist or environmental club what kind of butterflies are in your area and what plants attract them. Don't forget to find out what plants caterpillars eat (a critical element of your garden).

• **Pick a location for the garden.** It should be in a warm, sunny area sheltered from harsh winds, and away from the main pathway. Arrange your plants so that they create shade and protect the garden from wind— taller plants in the back of your garden, medium plants in the middle, and short plants in the front.

• **Make sure the area is free of pesticides.** If you've sprayed recently, wait three months before you plant your garden.

• **Provide a water source for the butterflies**—birdbaths, saucers of water, or drip irrigation systems work fine.

• **Start a community butterfly garden.** Start one in the corner of an existing community garden, at your church, at a local school, in a public park, or maybe even near the library.

RESOURCES

• **Butterfly Gardening** (Self Help Sheet #7) $2.50. The Xerces Society, 10 S.W. Ash St., Portland, OR 97204. *The Xerces Society is a nonprofit butterfly conservation organization. Send an SASE to get a list of other titles and membership information.*

• **Butterfly Gardening: Creating Summer Magic In Your Garden.** $18.95 *An expanded edition of the above book. 192 pages, including full color photographs. Check your bookstore, or order from the Xerces Society.*

• **The Butterfly Garden,** by Matthew Tekulsky. Harvard Common Press, Cambridge, MA. (617) 495-2577. *Includes information on raising butterflies from the larvae stage.*

The City of Baltimore, Maryland won't buy rainforest wood for city government use.

8. ALL THIS, AND CO$_2$

Electric utilities generate 28% of the
U.S. annual CO$_2$ emissions.

BACKGROUND. Have you every wondered what effect you, as an individual, are having on global warming? An Australian group called "The Greenhouse Association" recently came up with a simple formula to help you find out. It's on the next page.

All you need in order to estimate your impact on the greenhouse effect is a calculator, gas receipts, and your utility bills.

FUELED AGAIN

• Here's a way to understand the greenhouse effect: Think of a car parked in the summer sun. It gets incredibly hot inside because windows let the sunlight in, but don't let heat escape. Our atmosphere is like that. It naturally keeps the earth warm by trapping some of the sun's heat with a blanket of gases.

• The "recipe" for this blanket calls for fairly exact portions of water vapor, carbon dioxide (CO$_2$), methane, and a few others. They each trap a fraction of the heat escaping from the Earth. It's a delicate balance; too much of any one of them causes the atmosphere to get too hot.

• We've begun to upset that balance by burning vast quantities of fossil fuels—oil, coal, and natural gas—which release CO$_2$ into the atmosphere. In fact, because of fossil fuels, the atmosphere now contains 25% more CO$_2$ than it did a century ago.

• Scientists don't know exactly how much hotter this extra CO$_2$ will make the Earth. But many agree it will warm the Earth overall by 4° to 9° F by the year 2050. This could have disastrous effects. It could melt part of the polar ice caps, raising the sea level by a few feet, and flooding many of the world's major cities and harbors.

• Each of us is responsible for contributing to the greenhouse effect. We use fossil fuels when we drive, turn on the heat at home, use electricity, and burn wood.

YOUR GREENHOUSE REPORT CARD

• **You'll need your latest utility bill and gas credit card bill....and a calculator.** The calculations you'll be making are pretty simple, but a calculator will make them even easier. If you don't have a gasoline credit card, save your gasoline receipts for one month.

• **Find out how much energy you used last month.** Look on your gas credit card to find out how much gas you bought, and check your utility bill to find out how many "kilowatt-hours" (kwh) you used. If you have a natural gas bill, find out how many "therms" you used last month. (Kilowatt hours and therms are just the units your utility uses to measure your energy use.)

• Now use this chart to estimate the amount of CO_2 you released.

Electricity: _____ (kwh)	X	1.8	=	_____ lbs. of CO_2
Natural Gas: _____ (therms)	X	12	=	_____ lbs. of CO_2
Gasoline: _____ (gallons)	X	19	=	_____ lbs. of CO_2
Wood: _____ (pounds)	X	1.9	=	_____ lbs. of CO_2

TOTAL PER MONTH   =   lbs. of CO_2

• **How can you cut back on the amount of energy you use?** Now that you know your impact on the greenhouse effect, put your knowledge to work, and conserve energy. Keep track of how you're doing.

• Here's a hint: for every gallon of gas a car burns, it puts 18-20 lbs. of CO_2 into the atmosphere. It's hard to believe, but it's true.

RESOURCES

• *30 Simple Energy Things You Can Do to Save the Earth.* By the EarthWorks Group, published by EarthWorks Press, 1400 Shattuck Ave. #25, Berkeley, CA 94709. $4.95 postpaid. *This book on energy conservation was originally written for electric utilities. Check with your local utility to see if they offer it to customers for free.*

• **Greenhouse Action Packet.** Local Solutions to Global Pollution, 2121 Bonar St., Studio A, Berkeley, CA 94702. $6.

Experts speculate that some 50,000 kinds of plants may vanish during the next 30 years.

9. THE BALLOT OF THE GREEN BRIGADES

In 1988, there were 170 million possible voters in the U.S. Only 52% of them actually voted.

BACKGROUND. If you're looking for a way to make a difference, the voting booth is the place to start. Electing candidates who believe in protecting the environment is critically important.

If you're not registered to vote, or if you've recently moved and haven't re-registered, this should be a priority.

COUNTING VOTES

• Voting locally makes a difference nationally. Many environmental policies—e.g., community recycling laws—get their start on the local level before being adopted by state and federal governments.

• In 1960, John F. Kennedy was elected president by less than one vote per precinct. If only a handful of voters in each town hadn't bothered to vote that day, he wouldn't have made it to office.

• An initiative known as Forests Forever, which would have protected California's redwoods, was defeated in 1990. If just 13 more people per precinct had gone out and voted "Yes," Forests Forever would have passed.

WHAT YOU CAN DO

• **Pick Up A Voter Registration Form.** Post offices usually have them, but you can also get them from the city clerk's office or the County Registrar of Voters. If you can't get to one of these offices, call them and have them mail you a form.

• **Check the deadlines.** Most states require registration at least 30 days before an election in order to vote…but some require registration up to 50 days in advance.

A ten-mile commute by bike requires 350 calories of energy, the amount in one bowl of rice.

10. EARTH CONTROL

The world population has more than doubled since 1950.

BACKGROUND. Many people consider overpopulation a major environmental concern. "The reason we're in an eco-crisis," one person wrote to us, "is because we're straining the Earth's ability to support life. There are just too many human beings."

Whether you agree with this viewpoint or not, the issue is too large to ignore. It's important for each of us to understand the impact population growth is having on the environment.

PEOPLE
• Take a breath; three more babies were just born on the earth.

• Environmental Impact: 16,000 people are born every hour, 90% of them in developing countries.

• By the time an American reaches 75, he or she will have produced 52 tons of garbage, used 10 million gallons of water, and used five times as much energy as the world average.

RESOURCES
• **Zero Population Growth (ZPG),** 1400 16th St. NW, Ste. 320, Washington, DC 20036. (202) 332-2200. *ZPG is the largest American membership organization involved in world population and its impact on the environment. Call or write for information.*

• **Population-Environment Balance,** 1325 G Street, NW, Suite 1003, Washington, DC 20005. (202) 879-3000. *This group focuses on population stabilization as a means of safeguarding the environment. Call or write for information.*

• **Population Card / Calculator,** United Nations Bookstore, GA32, New York, NY 10017. (800) 553-3210. *This card is a small computer the size of a calculator. It calculates the population of the Earth every minute of every day until December 31, 2020. $21.*

In 1989, Americans threw away enough aluminum cans to build 6,000 DC-10 airplanes.

11. ENVIRONMENTAL NUTS

*Close to 55,000 square miles of rainforest are destroyed
each year—an area the size of New York State.*

BACKGROUND. A growing number of products use nuts,
leaves, and other materials that can be harvested from rainforests without threatening their survival. It's up to us to provide the market for those products.

TREES OF LIFE

• More than 1700 species of birds inhabit the rainforests in
Colombia alone, compared to 700 species on the entire continent
of North America.

• More than 25% of prescription drugs are derived from rainforest
materials. Rainforest plants and animals are the sources of drugs
that lower blood pressure, treat Parkinson's disease, treat glaucoma,
inhibit cancer cell growth, etc.

• Massive deforestation, combined with the spread of disease,
threatens an estimated 1,000 tribes of indigenous people with ex-
tinction.

• Sustainability pays. Scientists estimate that the sustainable boun-
ty of the forest is worth twice as much in the long run as the timber
that can be logged or the cattle that can be raised there.

WHAT YOU CAN DO
Shop Around

• Check out stores and catalogs. Look for products that come from
the fruits of the rainforest, but don't depend on cutting down trees.
As you find them, spread the word.

WHAT'S AVAILABLE?

• **Nuts.** Brazil nuts are one of the major cash-crops that grow natu-

More than 150 toxic waste dumps line the banks of the Niagara River...in one three-mile stretch▶

rally in the rainforest. Ben & Jerry's Rainforest Crunch—available as a candy or an ice cream—uses them. So do nut mixes packaged by From the Rainforest.

• **Oils.** The Body Shop, a British-based cosmetics company, is developing a line of skin- and hair-care products made from herbs and plants gathered in the rainforest.

• **Hats.** When many of his friends admired—and even coveted—his Latin American straw hat, made from the leaves of rainforest plants, Stefan Schinzinger began importing them. The fedora-style straw hat, braided by Guatemalan Indians, is available through Gardener's Supply (800 548-4784). Another of his models, the Palmata, is available through the Nature Company (800 227-1114).

• **Buttons.** Schinzinger also imports buttons made from the nuts of the Tagua palm—10 million buttons in 1990 alone. Useful as a substitute for ivory or plastic, they support a cottage industry in Ecuador. They're used by the North Face, Seventh Generation and others.

• **Land.** Several organizations make it their business to protect rainforests. Some buy land and protect it from logging, burning and ranching. Others help local residents replant the forest and take care of it. You won't get a product to put on your head or in your mouth, but it's still satisfying. Contact the groups below for info.

RESOURCES

• **Cultural Survival**, 53A Church St., Cambridge, MA 02138. (617) 495-2562. *Call for a list of rainforest products including cashews, Brazil nuts, soaps, bath oil, fruit, handicrafts.Free.*

• **Arbofilia**, Basic Foundation, P.O. Box 47012, St. Petersburg, FL 33743. *Arbofila is a project to help Costa Rican farmers plant tropical forest trees. A $5 donation will plant one tree. For information send a SASE. (800) 752-0668*

• **"Adopt-an-Acre Program"**.The Nature Conservancy, 1815 North Lynn St., Arlington, VA 22209.(800) 628-6860. *$30 protects an acre of rainforest...*

• **Rainforest Action Network**, 301, Suite A,San Francisco, CA 94133. *Send a SASE for a list of sustainable rainforest products.*

An average retrofit investment pays for itself in lower utility bills within 4 years.

12. HERE COMES THE SUN

Soldier's Grove, Wisconsin, adopted an ordinance requiring that the town's businesses get 50% of their heat from the sun.

BACKGROUND. Whatever happened to electric cars, wind power, and solar energy? They're still viable...and certain solar technologies are becoming more affordable. But there has to be more support and interest if they're ever going to reach their potential. Now is the time to learn more about alternative energy and find ways to make it part of your life.

DID YOU KNOW
• Experts say that at current consumption rates, the world's known oil reserves will be used up in 35 years.

• Burning fossil fuels is the main cause of the greenhouse effect. Switching to alternatives like solar energy will reduce global warming.

• Alternative energy technology is available today. The Solar Energy Research Institute estimates that as many as 60% of American homes receive enough sunlight to be retrofitted for some form of solar heating.

• Solar photovoltaics, cells that convert the energy of the sun into electricity, now account for about $175 million in annual sales with estimates that they will be a billion dollar industry by the mid-1990s.

• The best-selling solar-powered product? Americans bought more than two million solar-powered calculators last year.

WHAT YOU CAN DO
• **Read about it.** Solar will never gain acceptance if people don't know more about it.

• **Check out demonstrations or exhibits** of alternative energy. It's an opportunity to see alternative energy at work. Science museums, nature centers, or local utilities are likely places to find them.

An estimated 1.2 million homes in the U.S. use solar water systems.

- **Know Your Options.** Order some of the catalogs listed in the Resources section. The catalogs listed describe many of the renewable energy products available, ranging from wind generators and photovoltaic panels that can power televisions to solar powered flashlights and calculators.

- **Keep Your eyes open.** Technology keeps changing, so keep reading and watch for new applications and new products.

FOR MORE INFO

- **National Appropriate Technology Assistance Service** (NATAS), PO Box 2525, Butte, Montana 59702-2525, (800) 428-2525. *A public information phone line specializing in helping individuals and small businesses use renewable and other alternative energy sources.*

- **Conservation and Renewable Energy Inquiry and Referral Service** Box 8900, Silver Spring, Maryland 20907 (800) 523-2929. *Offers fact sheets and brochures on alcohol fuels solar, wind energy and bio-conversion.*

- **National Center for Appropriate Technology (NCAT)** PO Box 4000, Butte, Montana 59702. *Send for their list of publications including booklets on how to build your own breadbox solar water heater, or solar greenhouse, how to make fuel alcohol and more.*

- **Solar Energy Research Institute (SERI)**, 1617 Cole Blvd. Golden, Colorado 80401 (303) 231-1000

- **Passive Solar Industries Council,** 1090 Vermont Ave. NW #1200, Washington DC, 20005 (202) 371-0357.

- **Real Goods Sourcebook,** 966 Mazzoni St., Ukiah, CA 95482. (800) 762-7325. $14. *The bible of alternative energy products and technologies. Also have a free mail order catalog.*

- **Solar Electric / EarthOptions,** 116 4th St., Santa Rosa, CA 95401. (707) 542-1990. *Catalog of efficient and solar products, available for $3.50.*

- **Sunelco,** PO box 1499, G-11, Hamilton, MT 59840. (800)338-6844. *Catalog and planning guide, $. 4.00*

- **Photo Comm,** 930 Maryland Rd., Grass Valley, CA 95945. (800) 544-6466. *Write or call for catalog.*

- **Seventh Generation,** Colchester, VT 05446. (800) 456-1177. *Mail order catalog of products for a healthy planet.*

Solar electric cells are used to power call boxes on the San Diego Freeway.

13. ADOPT A PIECE OF THE PLANET

The Trust For Public Land can protect nearly $10 of rainforest land for every dollar you donate.

BACKGROUND. Wilderness and undeveloped land are disappearing all over the world.

Don't you wish you could do something about it? Wishing alone can't do it...but dollars can. There are organizations which buy and preserve all the open land they can afford. Your money will help support their efforts.

THIS LAND IS YOUR LAND

• According to the World Resources Institute, between 40 and 50 million acres of the earth's forests are destroyed every year—that's about 80 acres every minute.

• Tropical deforestation releases as much as 2 billion tons of carbon dioxide, a greenhouse gas, into the air every year. Buying rainforest land prevents deforestation and reduces the greenhouse effect.

• American land is being protected, too. For example: The Nature Conservancy recently bought a 30,000 acre ranch in Oklahoma and created the Tallgrass Prarie Preserve, where it plans to reintroduce more than 1,500 bison to the prairie.

• Conservation International is involved in "debt for nature swaps." They offer Third World countries a chance to wipe out some debts. In exchange, the countries agree to put money into local wilderness preservation.

WHAT YOU CAN DO

• Ask groups for examples of their projects, and decide which ones you'd like to support. Find out how much of your money is actually

About 90% of the energy that businesses use, worldwide, comes from burning fossil fuels.

spent on the projects. Every charitable organization uses some of its donations to pay for overhead expenses....But how much?

• There may also be groups involved in local preservation projects. If you aren't able to donate money, you can still make a difference: Donate your time. An afternoon or weekend spent helping them with their projects will be as valuable to them as money.

RESOURCES

• **The Nature Conservancy,** 1815 N. Lynn St., Arlington, VA 22209(800) 628-6860. *They have local offices in every state—call or write to get the address one near you.$30 protects an acre of rainforest through the Nature Conservancy's Adopt-an-Acre Program. For info send a SASE.*

• **Trust for Public Land,** 116 New Montgomery, 4th flr, San Francisco, CA 94105. (415) 495-4014. *They purchase land for public use, also help community groups set up land trusts to buy land.*

The Sears Tower in Chicago has the a/c going even when outdoor temperatures are below zero.

14. COMPLETE THE CYCLE

This is the part of recycling people often overlook.

BACKGROUND. You may think you're recycling because you've taken your bins full of bottles and cans to the recycling center. You are—but that's only part of it.

Manufacturers have to do something with the materials you send back to them. The most environmentally sound option is to use the materials to make new products.

There's one catch: there has to be demand for the recycled goods.

That's where you come in. . .again. After all, if you don't buy items made from recycled materials, who will?

DID YOU KNOW

• According to the Institute for Local Self-Reliance "Re-use saves 90-99% of the materials consumed in making a product from virgin materials."

• Buying recycled reduces pollution. For example, when a steel mill uses recycled scrap, it cuts related water pollution, air pollution and mining wastes by 70%. Using recycled aluminum cuts related pollution by as much as 95%.

• Every ton of recycled paper Americans buy saves 17 trees, 7,000 gallons of water, and enough energy to heat and air-condition a five room house for six months.

• In the last two years, the number of companies making products out of recycled materials has increased more than ten times and the number of recycled products available has increased even more— from 170 recycled products to over 2,400.

RE-PURCHASING POWER

• **See what's available.** Remember when the only thing you could buy recycled was writing paper? That's changed. Now you can get recycled motor oil, greeting cards, toilet paper, office products, even high-fashion handbags and jewelry made from old tires.

Americans throw away 900,000 oils filters each day.

•**Find out where to get it.** Check the stores where you normally shop. There are also a growing number of places that specialize in recycled products; call a local environmental group to see if they can direct you to one. Another alternative: If you still can't find what you're looking for, many environmental products catalogs sell recycled products.

Note: Some recycled products cost a little more than unrecycled ones. However, higher costs are almost always the result of a weak market. When you—and others—begin buying recycled products on a regular basis, the prices will drop.

"RECYCLED" VS. "RECYCLABLE"

• **Know what's what.** Manufacturers want you to believe their products are good for the earth—but read the fine print. "Recycled" products are made either partly or completely of recycled materials. But as we mentioned elsewhere, "Recyclable" simply means materials *can* be recycled *if* there's somewhere in your area that will take them.

• **Look for the words "post-consumer."** That means products are made from materials that people have actually used—as opposed to reprocessed factory leftovers.

• **Be an Activist—get stores to stock recycled products.** If local stores don't carry recycled products, encourage them to start.

• **Write to manufacturers.** If enough of us write to them, they'll see that there's a market for recycled products—and start to make changes.

RESOURCES

• *"Buy Recycled—a Consumer Products Guide,"* Californians Against Waste Foundation, 909 12th St., Sacramento, CA 95814. $3. *Also have a guide to recycled writing and printing paper.*

• **Conservatree Information Services.** 10 Lombard St., Suite 250, San Francisco, CA 94111. *Their "Greenline" newsletter subscription entitles you to six bimonthly newsletters and many other materials involving recycled paper issues. Send a SASE to get more information, or subscribe for $29.00.*

Americans buy 140 million gallons of latex paint each year.

15. DOLLARS & SENSE

Americans have invested more than $500 billion in
environmentally oriented and socially responsible corporations.

BACKGROUND. If you're like most people, you probably don't have any money invested directly in the stock market—only about 20% of Americans do. But most likely your city, county and state governments own stocks, and so does your pension fund.

You have a voice in how these funds are invested. Put it to work for the environment.

DID YOU KNOW

• The Calvert Social Investment Fund refuses to buy stock in companies that produce CFC's, toxic pesticides, and that violate federal, state, or local environmental laws. Company surveys have shown that its 40,000 investors have made the environment their number-one concern among a number of social issues.

• One fund, the New Alternatives Fund, invests exclusively in companies that work on alternative energy sources, recycling, pollution cleanup, and energy conservation.

• Pension funds own $1.3 trillion worth of stock in U.S. corporations, including more than 50% of the outstanding stocks in America's largest corporations.

• AT&T and Lotus Software offer an environmental investment alternatives for members of their retirement plan. Ben and Jerry's pension investments are entirely screened by the Calvert Fund.

FUND FACTS

• In the aftermath of the Exxon *Valdez* oil spill, the Coalition for Environmentally Responsible Economies (CERES), a group of environmental organizations and investment groups, formulated an environmental code of conduct called the Valdez Principles for corporations to follow.

• The Valdez Principles require corporations to commit to

Three mature trees can remove up to 50 lbs. of CO_2 from the air each year.

reducing waste, disclosing hazards, performing environmental audits, and other environmental standards. Right now only 21 smaller companies have agreed to abide by the Valdez Principles, but a number of Fortune 500 companies are currently discussing the principles with CERES.

• The stock market has shown that careful environmental investing can work. In 1990, The Eco-Logical Trust 1990 and the Progressive Environmental Fund, two environmental mutual funds, outperformed the Dow Jones industrial average and other major stock market indicators.

WHAT YOU CAN DO

• If you own stocks, consider adding to your portfolio stocks of companies that adhere to the Valdez principles, and selling stocks with poor environmental records. Contact Progressive Asset Management or another broker to get information on firms you're thinking of investing in.

• Encourage your local government to establish investment policies that adhere to the Valdez Principles. The Comptroller of New York City and the California State Controller's Office have already adopted the Valdez guidelines.

• Find out if your company offers an environmental pension fund alternative. It it does, consider moving your pension into the fund.

• If your company doesn't, lobby the board of directors of your pension fund director to make one available to employees.

RESOURCES

•**Coalition for Environmentally Responsible Economies (CERES)**, 711 Atlantic Ave, Boston, MA 02111. (617) 451-3436. *Call or write for a guide to the Valdez Principles and assistance in promoting the adoption of environmental investment policies by pension funds and local governments.*

•**Progressive Asset Management, Inc.**, 1814 Franklin St., Oakland, CA 94612. 1-800-586-2998. *The first full-service securities broker to specialize in socially and environmentally responsible investments. Contact them to receive a guide to environmentally responsible investing, including mutual funds, individual securities, and portfolio managers.*

Kids age 6-11 in Freeport, Maine, convinced their town council to ban Styrofoam.

16. THE AGE OF RESIN

*It takes 1,050 recycled milk jugs to
make a six-foot plastic park bench.*

BACKGROUND. People want to know why more plastic isn't being recycled. In some cases it's because recycling plastic doesn't make economic sense—it's cheaper (and maybe even more energy-efficient) to make new plastic. In other cases, it's because American recycling is still in its early stages.

Of course, "To recycle or not to recycle?" may not be the question at all. Some environmentalists think that the real solution isn't to *recycle* plastic, but to use a lot less of it.

Either way, we have to do something—we're currently throwing away more than 15 million tons of plastic every year.

So what can you do? The first thing is to learn the difference between plastics. There are seven common types, and they *can't* be recycled together.

In fact, the seventh type—a mixture of different plastics, can't be recycled at all.

DID YOU KNOW

• Most plastic bottles are made of a material called high-density polyethylene—HDPE for short. In 1988, we used 2 billion lbs. of HDPE just to make household bottles. And less than 1% of it was recycled.

• Plastic in soft drink bottles, known as PET or PETE (short for polyethylene terephthalate) are actually a form of polyester. They aren't usually recycled into more bottles, but they are used to make carpet, fiberfill for sleeping bags and winter jackets, and polyester suits. (It takes 26 bottles to make a suit.)

• PET bottles are the most recycled plastic. According to *Modern Plastics* Magazine, we recycled 20% of them in 1989.

• According to *Garbage* Magazine, it took more than 22 million

Less than 5% of the total land area in the U.S. is considered wilderness.

barrels of oil and 34 million cubic feet of natural gas to make the plastic packaging we used in America in 1989.

WHAT YOU CAN DO
Pick a Number.
So consumers can tell which plastic is which, the plastics industry is beginning to label containers with code numbers. Look for a number from 1-7 inside a recycling symbol stamped on the bottom of each item. But don't be misled by the symbol—it really has nothing to do with whether the product has already been recycled...or whether it can even be recycled in your area. Here are the numbers:

• **#1** is PETE (polyethylene terephthalate). In addition to plastic soda bottles, it's used to make peanut butter jars, mouthwash bottles, and other containers.

• **#2** is HDPE (high-density polyethylene). It's used in milk jugs, detergent bottles, motor oil containers, etc. Some curbside programs and recycling centers take it.

• **#3** is PVC (polyvinyl chloride). It's used in credit cards, shampoo bottles, cooking oil bottles, water bottles, etc. Very little is ever recycled.

• **#4** is LDPE (low-density polyethylene). It's used primarily in shrink wrap and plastic bags.

• **#5** is polypropylene. It's used in plastic bottle caps and lids, drinking straws, yogurt and cottage cheese containers, etc.

• **#6** is polystyrene and polystyrene foam. It's use primarily for food containers, cups, packing "peanuts," meat trays, etc.

• **#7** is mixed plastic—several kinds sandwiched or mixed together. None of them are recyclable.

The plastics recycling situation is different in every community. To find out what can and can't be recycled in your area, call a local recycling center.

Only 5% of Americans use public transportation to get to work.

17. GROW NATIVE

You don't have to go to the rainforest to protect endangered species. You can save them in your own backyard.

BACKGROUND. Because we've cultivated so many exotics, we've overlooked the value of preserving native plants. They're important to the eco-system—not only for their beauty, but because they support wildlife and are much better-suited to the climate and soil conditions than imports. We need to protect and grow them.

SEEDS FOR THOUGHT

• Native plants in your garden take less water, less fertilizer...and less of your time.

• Learn about local wild plants and animals. Contact habitat restoration groups in your area. Use the "Resources" to find them.

RESOURCES
• **The National Wildflower Research Center Clearinghouse.** 2600 FM 973 North, Austin, TX 78725. *They'll supply a wildflower list, addresses of nearby native plant nurseries, and sources for wild seeds for any state in the U.S. Cost: $3. You can also send $9.95 to order their "Wildflower Handbook."*

• **Attracting Backyard Wildlife: A guide for nature lovers,** by Bill Merilees. Voyageur Press, 123 North Second St., Stillwater, Minnesota. Cost: $14.95 postpaid.

• **Prairie Nursery,** PO Box 306, Westfield, WI 53964. (608) 296-3679. *A catalog for wildflower seeds and nursery-propagated wild plants, so you don't have to disturb natural areas. $3.*

• **The Society for Ecological Restoration.** University of Wisconsin Arboretum, 1207 Seminole Highway, Madison WI 53711. *An organization of professional and amateur ecological restorers. They'll refer you to organizations in your area interested in habitat restoration.*

The average car pumps its own weight in CO_2 into the atmosphere every year.

18. LEAVE HOME WITHOUT IT

Americans drive the distance to the planet Pluto and back every day.

B ACKGROUND. One of the best things you can do for the environment is to use your car less. So we suggest you try a regular "No-Car Day" once a month...or once a week. Who knows—it might become a habit.

DID YOU KNOW

• According to Greenpeace Action, "cars are the biggest source of greenhouse gases and the largest single cause of ozone smog."

• *In These Times* reports: "There are more than 180 million motor vehicles in this country—an increase of 25 million since 1980. Four out of every five miles in the U.S. are traveled by car. "

• Since 1970, the amount of miles driven increased 72%...and the U.S. Federal Highway Administration predicts another 50% increase by the year 2000.

• In American cities, close to half the urban space goes to accommodate cars; in Los Angeles, the figure is two-thirds.

• According to Environmental Action, "the high octane gas used to power many high-performance cars contains some of the most deadly chemicals known, including toluene, and xylene, which form benzene when burned. Benzene is one of the five most dangerous toxic chemicals found in the air. It is present in elevated levels in the air of many states...and 85% of it comes from gasoline."

WHAT YOU CAN DO

• If you can just stop driving one day a week, do it. If you can't, here's a way to ease into it: For a week, write down where you drive, and why. Look your list over—can you eliminate one day's worth of trips? For example, can you take the bus, combine trips, or do errands with a friend in one car?

Since Europeans first settled in the U.S., nearly 50% of our wetlands have been destroyed.

FOR YOUR

NEIGHBORS

19. CHECK OUT YOUR LIBRARY

There are more than 15,000 libraries in the United States.

BACKGROUND. Chances are, your library already has public information programs. But do they cover environmental issues? And is there a good selection of environmental books and magazines? Why not volunteer at the library... and work with librarians to make sure environmental information is available to everyone in your community.

DID YOU KNOW
• Libraries are community centers. The American Library Association estimates that 58% of all Americans go to public libraries each year. In Chicago more than half a million people use the public library in a single month.

• Even more impressive: 42 million students visit libraries every week.

• According to the American Library Association, 61% of U.S. public libraries depend on volunteer support.

WHAT YOU CAN DO
• **Work with librarians** to set up an environmental display—a collection of books and other materials on a table where they can be easily seen.

• **Make an environmental bulletin board.** Post notices about community environmental services, classes, children's programs, etc.

• **Start a "green magazine" fund.** People can sign up to help pay for subscriptions of environmental magazines.

• **Set up an environmental speaker program.** Find speakers at community colleges, environmental groups, local nature groups.

Over 100 cities have enacted legislation limiting the use of polystyrene foam.

20. BE CHAIRMAN OF THE BOARD

*Commuters waste enough gasoline in traffic jams every year
to drive to the sun and back more than 300 times.*

BACKGROUND. Your car's stuck in traffic. You're late for work again. And on top of everything else, the price of gas has gone up. Why are you doing this to yourself? You could start a ridesharing project at your company. All it takes is a map, a bulletin board, and a few push-pins.

DID YOU KNOW
• Most cars on the road carry only one person. In fact, we have so much extra room in our 140 million cars that everyone in Western Europe could ride in them with us.

• It has been reported that 50% of the smog in most metropolitan areas is caused by automobile emissions.

• Commuters spent 2 billion hours stuck in traffic jams last year— and wasted about 3 billion gallons of gasoline in the process. That's been estimated at about 5% of our entire annual gasoline use.

WHAT YOU CAN DO
• Match up people in your company who live near each other, so they can rideshare. Here's how:

• Put up a large map of the surrounding area on a bulletin board. Give each employee a push-pin. Ask each to write his or her name and phone number on a small piece of paper, and pin it on the map to show where each of them lives.

• List people who live near each other, and distribute the list to your co-workers.

• Ask your employer to provide incentives to encourage ridesharing. One idea: Give carpoolers free parking spaces, and charge solo commuters a fee to park.

90% of new American cars are air-conditioned.

21. GOT A LIGHT?

Replacing a standard light bulb with a compact fluorescent bulb saves the energy equivalent of 600 lbs. of coal over the life of the bulb.

BACKGROUND. You're wandering through a store looking for a low-flow showerhead or an energy-saving light bulb. You can't find one, so you ask for help. Unfortunately, the clerks don't know what you're talking about. And the manager doesn't either.

Frustrated? You're probably not alone. How can anyone in your community buy energy or water-saving fixtures if they can't even find them?

Why not turn your local hardware store into an environmental supply center? Retail stores supply what their customers want. So let them know what you want.

DID YOU KNOW

• The U.S. currently imports more than 50% of its oil, more than in the oil crisis of the 1970s—and imports are expected to rise in the future. Much of this is used to generate residential electricity—so making homes more energy-efficient reduces our dependence on foreign oil and helps the economy.

• The average American home wastes much of the energy it consumes. Energy-efficient household products help cut down emissions responsible for acid rain, the greenhouse effect, and other environmental ills.

• Surveys show that 90% of Americans would rather buy water- and energy-saving products at a local store than order them by phone or mail. But one manufacturer of quality water conservation products told us that only 2% of his sales are through retail stores—despite his efforts to get stores to carry his line.

SHOPPING SURVEY

• The next time you go to a hardware store, check to see how many energy- and water-saving products it carries. Take notes as you go. Bring along environmental catalogues to help you look for

The carbon emissions from oil, coal, and natural gas energy sources in 1989: 5,764 tons.

specific products and brand names. Pay attention to how well displayed the products are.

Check the Store for These Items:

• **Plumbing:** Low-flow showerheads (2.5 gallons per minute or less), ultra low-flush toilets, toilet dams, and water-saving faucet aerators.

• **Lighting:** Compact fluorescent lightbulbs, energy-saving flood-lights, and energy-efficient outdoor fixtures (such as metal halide, high pressure sodium or compact fluorescent).

• **Miscellaneous:** Water heater insulating jackets, appliance timers, programmable thermostats, battery rechargers, and weather-stripping supplies.

HARDWARE AUDIT

• List what you were looking for, what the store had, and what it didn't have. Compare the selection with other local hardware stores. Make a separate list for each store.

• If one store had a better selection than the others, let each of the managers know, and tell them that you and your friends will shop at the store with the best selection.

• Make good on your promise—change your shopping habits. Shop at the store that has the best selection of goods and encourage others to do the same.

• Contact your local energy or water utility; find out if they offer rebate coupons for conservation products. If they do, ask them to provide local hardware stores with stand-up displays. Using rebates makes energy-saving products more affordable.

RESOURCES

• **Baubiologie Hardware Catalog,** *200 Palo Colorado Canyon Rd., Carmel, CA 93923, (800) 441-8971.*

• **Ecologue,** by Bruce Anderson (Prentice Hall,1990). *A book that lists a variety of products and manufacturers.*

• **The Energy Store,** PO Box 3507, Santa Cruz, CA 95063-3507 (800) 288-1938. *Energy and water saving products for the home.*

• **Ecological Water Products,** 266 Main St., Suite 18, Dept GM Medfield, MA 02052; (800) 926-NOVA. *Free brochure.*

According to Worldwatch, U.S. oil imports skyrocketed 60% over the past 6 years.

22. BE A MAPMAKER

More than 10,000 copies of the East Bay Conservation Corps' Recycling Guide have been distributed in Alameda County, California, since 1989.

BACKGROUND. How long have you put off cleaning up your basement or attic because you didn't want to throw out your "usable junk" …but didn't know what else to do with it? Your neighbors may be in the same boat. Here's a creative way to help them—and yourself—recycle old things, and get to know your community a little better at the same time: Draw up a map of places where things can be recycled in your area…and get it distributed.

DID YOU KNOW

• On the average, Americans recycle only about 10% of our trash. Compare that with European countries, which recycle as much as 60%.

• In a recent survey, 43% of the people who don't recycle said they would try it if they knew where their local recycling centers were.

WHAT YOU CAN DO

Before You Start

• Decide what area to cover. Your map can cover a whole county, a town, or just a neighborhood.

• You can limit the map to "official" recycling centers, or add places where second-hand merchandise is sold. For example: flea markets, salvage yards, used book stores, etc. Find them in the Yellow Pages.

• Remember: The bigger the area and the more outlets you include, the more legwork will be necessary.

•Check with a local library or city government for a map you can copy. Note: Many commercially produced maps are copyrighted.

The city of Baltimore has purchased recycled paper to replace foam products.

Visit stores and recycling facilities

• Pinpoint their locations, verify that they're reputable, and find out basic information about what goods they accept, how much they pay, when they're open, etc.

• Ask for permission to list them.

Make a Map

• Include names, addresses and phone numbers of each store or recycling center.

• Ask local photocopy centers if they'd be willing to donate the printing in return for "co-sponsorship" of the map (and a printed credit). If not, try for a discount.

• Alternative: Approach your local Chamber of Commerce, city Community Services Dept., or other civic group and ask if they'll participate...and help support costs.

Distribute It

• Sell it as part of a community project—e.g., for school fundraisers—or as a commercial venture.

• If you can afford it, drop them off at the library, PTA, or other community group meetings.

• If your city government is sponsoring the map, they'll come up with ways of getting it into the community.

• Ask your local newspaper or Yellow Pages publisher to print it.

RESOURCES

• **Local Solutions to Global Pollution**, 2121 Bonar St., Studio A, Berkeley, CA 94702. *They'll send you a copy of the recycling map distributed by the city of Albany, CA. It's a good sample. You MUST send a self-addressed, stamped envelope to receive a map.*

1/4 of the grapes eaten in the U.S. are grown 7,000 miles away, in Chile.

23. WHAT'S GREEN & READ ALL OVER?

Green Cross, a labeling program based in Oakland, California, is already working with more than 800 grocery stores on the West Coast.

BACKGROUND. You're cruising the aisles of your local grocery store, and you stop to look at your shopping list. Let's see...You'd like to buy a "green" laundry soap, but which one is it? If your supermarket supported a green labeling program, it would be easy to tell.

Every supermarket should provide educational materials to its customers, to help us make the right environmental choices every time we shop.

DID YOU KNOW

• Every year, 10-15,000 new products are introduced onto supermarket shelves. That's a lot of items to keep track of. A recent survey found that nearly 80% of us have changed our buying habits because of environmental concerns.

• But it's frustrating—there's not enough information about who the "good guys" are. In another survey, over half the people polled said they were aware of companies that have damaged the environment...but only 14% said they could remember any positive environmental advertising.

• Green labeling works. Whatever the product, shoppers *will* make ecologically sound purchases if a store can show them how. In Germany, the government's paint-labeling program has kept 40,000 tons of solvents from being dumped into the waste stream.

• National labeling programs are in operation in Japan, Canada and throughout Europe.

WHAT YOU CAN DO

• **Check supermarkets in your area.** Which one is the most environmentally sensitive? Do any already provide educational materi-

300 bills relating to packaging were introduced in state legislatures in 1990.

als about green products? If so, consider shopping there regularly.

• If none do, or if you still prefer a store that *doesn't* offer materials, educate them.

• Talk to the manager. Give him or her some information about green labeling and explain that many people in your community want to know which products are "green"—but the items aren't easy to identify in that store. Note: Start saving your grocery receipts a few weeks before you visit the store. Use them to show how much business you represent.

• Tell them that the two major green labeling programs—Green Seal and Green Cross—provide educational materials for stores to hand out to customers.

• If the store manager doesn't show any interest, consider a petition. Best place to gather signatures: right outside the store.

GETTING GREEN

• What are green labeling programs? Two independent organizations—Green Cross and Green Seal—research and certify products based on different levels of environmental impact.

• If you write them for information, they can use your letter as an example of consumer interest.

RESOURCES

• **Green Seal,** 1875 Connecticut Ave., NW, Ste. 300A, Washington, DC 20009. *They have a brochure available on what the labels in stores mean.* Send SASE. Free.

• **Green Cross Certification Company,** Consumer Affairs, 1611 Telegraph Ave., Suite 1111, Oakland, CA 94612 (800) 829-1416. (415) 832-1415. *They can tell you which supermarkets in your area are involved, which products they endorse, and how to get green labeling in your supermarket.*

Recreational boaters dispose of 421,371 tons of garbage in U.S. waters a year.

24. GREEN PTA

*The PTA was founded in February, 1897, as
the National Congress of Mothers.*

BACKGROUND. The PTA is a powerful organization—one
of the most respected voices in America. So when the PTA
puts its muscle behind an issue like protecting the planet, it's
going to make a difference.

Get involved at school. Make your local PTA an advocate for
environmental education.

DID YOU KNOW

• The PTA has more than 27,000 local chapters and 6.8 million
members nationwide—that's about one PTA member for every sev-
en schoolchildren in America.

• It may seem like a stodgy organization to some people, but it
isn't. The PTA has been politically active throughout its 94-year
history. It played a major role in implementing the first child labor
laws, promoting special education programs, and improving school
libraries. And it can do the same for the environment.

• For example, the PTA of Davis Elementary, Georgia, generated
over $2,000 through recycling projects and reinvested it in educa-
tional environmental programs, endangered species adoptions, and
habitat developments at their school

PTA PROJECTS

• Find out who else in your local PTA is interested in working on
environmental projects. Set up a "green committee"; work with
them to plan activities for your school.

• Set up a recycling program at your school—and use the money
you raise to support environmental education. Aluminum, glass,
and newspaper drives are a good place to start.

One tree absorbs about 50 lbs. of CO_2 each year.

- Convert part of your schoolyard into a nature area. Raise plants native to your area, create a butterfly garden, or even raise wild flowers.
- Organize a tree planting day.
- Develop activities that teach children about endangered animals and plants.
- Collect and distribute materials that kids can use to make recycling bins for their homes.
- Organize field trips to landfills or manufacturing plants that make things from recycled materials.

For the teachers

- Make a "green classroom" checklist. List things that students and teachers can do in the classroom to save energy, recycle materials, raise native plants, and other projects.
- Make an environmental "fact file" that teachers can use to integrate the environment into their lessons. Clip newspaper and magazine articles, compile lists of books at the library, and prepare fact sheets and resource lists.

Let other parents know

- Put an environmental section in your PTA's bulletin to keep parents informed about your projects. Even if they don't participate in the PTA, they may be interested in some of the activities.

Contact other PTA chapters to see what they've done

- Call other schools in your area, and the state and national PTA headquarters to share experiences and get ideas for more projects.

RESOURCES

- **PTA World Headquarters,** 700 North Rush, Chicago, IL 60611. (312) 787-0977

WARNING: Even "natural" pesticides are deadly to butterflies.

25. STARRING AVID GARDENER

A 100-square-foot community garden can produce 10,000 servings of produce in a year.

BACKGROUND. Whether you're an avid gardener, or someone who just wishes you had the time and place to start a garden, this is a wonderful project. It creates community spirit, gives you a chance to get to know your neighbors, and offers a "hands-on" opportunity to work with the Earth.

DID YOU KNOW

• Many states don't regulate organic farming, so you may not know what's in the produce you buy—even if it says "Organic." By growing your own you can guarantee that what you're eating is pesticide-free.

• Eighty-two percent of pesticides registered with the EPA leave residues on food; 11% show at least "limited evidence" of being carcinogenic.

• Nancy Skinner, a Berkeley naturalist, says that "Gardens preserve green, open space in overpaved urban areas. They not only help clean the air, they serve as a reminder that there are other things in the world besides cars, streets, and buildings."

• Gardens are possible anywhere. According to Boston Urban Gardeners, "Carrie Sargent, resident of a drug- and crime-torn section of Boston, had a vision to create a community garden. She worked to have one of the many empty lots on her street, a site for illegal dumping, crime, and abandoned and stolen cars, purchased by a local nonprofit organization to turn into a garden....Today it's a flourishing community garden, a safe, beautiful place for neighbors to meet and grow food together."

Vanpooling fact: A full van removes 13 cars from traffic.

START A COMMUNITY GARDEN

• **Get people involved.** According to one expert, you need a core of 3-5 people to start a community garden and see it through. Find out which of your friends or neighbors are interested.

Choose a Spot.

• Make it accessible to everyone. It could be in a backyard, an empty lot, even on church grounds or a utility easement.

• If you see a vacant lot you like, find out how to contact the owner and ask permission to use it. He or she may prefer a well-maintained garden to a weed-covered lot.

• If it's city property, there may be a program that encourages the use of vacant lots for community purposes. Ask City Hall.

• If you think the soil may have been contaminated by chemicals or pollution, get it tested. Call a nursery for details.

• Decide what to plant: flowers, vegetables, native plants...or some of each? Consider including native plants.

• Decide if the garden could be a food source for garden members or the community. For example, you could donate vegetables to a food pantry.

• Short on space? If you don't have enough room for a full garden, use planter boxes. They fit almost anywhere, and they're movable.

RESOURCES

• **The City Gardener's Handbook, by Linda Yang (Random House, Inc.) (800)733-3000** *Concentrates on the design of small city gardens, an aspect most beginning gardeners ignore.*

• **American Community Gardening Assn, 325 Walnut St., Philadelphia, PA 19106.** *Nationwide membership organization of community gardeners. They'll provide technical assistance to individuals and groups trying to set up their own community gardens.*

• *A Handbook of Community Gardening,* Boston Urban Gardeners, 46 Chestnut Ave., Jamaica Plain, MA 02130. $11.95.

•**Creating a Community Garden**, Minnesota Horticultural Society, 1970 Folwell, 161 Alderman Hall, St. Paul , MN 55108. $3.

26. GO TO
THE SOURCE

Tens of thousands of kids write to eco-groups every year for information.

B ACKGROUND. When kids ask about the greenhouse effect...or want to know what's being done to protect local wildlife, where can they go to learn more?

Wouldn't it be great if there were a comprehensive list that told you what opportunities were available in your area? If there isn't one already, it's because no one has compiled it yet.

How about you?

THEY'RE OUT THERE

• The Recyclones are a theater group that travel around the San Francisco area, teaching school children about recycling.

•The Sierra Club in NYC has a program called Inner City Outings. Inner city kids go to the woods for day hikes and overnights. The club arranges the funding.

• The Bay Model in Sausalito, California, is a 3/4-acre model of the San Francisco Bay and its ecology. They offer free tours to school kids in the fourth grade and up.

CREATE A KIDS' ENVIRONMENTAL
EDUCATIONAL RESOURCE GUIDE

• **Include:** ecology centers, bird watching, gardening classes, films, science museums, a field trip source list, etc.

• **To find them:** Call local environmental groups for suggestions. Chances are, they've done a lot of the research already.

• **Check with:** your town recreation department, the YMCA or YWCA, the public library, book stores.

• **Be creative.** List anything that even remotely applies, and let your readers make the choice.

• Your city government or chamber of commerce may sponsor your pamphlet. Local printing companies may be willing to print it for free (or give you a discount) in exchange for a mention.

27. IF YOU HAD A HAMMER...

The most popular tools at the Berkeley tool librarys are pruning tools.

BACKGROUND. Have you ever backed away from doing a project because the tools would have cost too much?

There's an alternative—a tool-lending library where every tool is available for the community to share. Promote conservation and this unique form of recycling—get your library to start a tool-lending program. Make our resources count.

TOOL DAYS

• The idea of library tool-lending programs isn't new. The public library in Grosse Point, Michigan, started with 28 tools in 1943—now it has over 2,000 items. From July 1989 to June 1990 it circulated over 1900 tools. According to the librarian, "The community loves it—it's been successful since the day it began."

• The public tool library in Berkeley, California, was set up in 1979. Its purpose was to provide tools for lower-income families. Borrowers can check out wrenches, drills, crowbars, even cement mixers. The library has 30-100 people stopping by every day. It costs them as little as a dollar to get what they need.

WHAT YOU CAN DO

• Contact the local library. Suggest they start a tool collection.

• Put together a seed group of people who support the idea and may be willing to donate tools.

• There may be community development funds you can use to buy tools and start the library. Other funding ideas: Contact a neighborhood improvement program or a Model Cities program.

• Contact local hardware stores to see if they'd be willing to donate tools.

• Ask local TV and radio stations to do public service announcements to get the word out as a "tool recycling" project.

San Diego County recycled 97,000 Christmas trees in 1988.

28. BE AN OZONE ACTIVIST

According to the NRDC, American companies are using more ozone-depleting chemicals now, despite awareness of ozone destruction.

BACKGROUND. How much more of the ozone layer can we afford to lose? According to some estimates, about 5% of it is already gone. Yet a lot of us continue to use ozone-depleting chemicals in everyday products. And stores keep selling them.

It's important to educate retailers about the causes of ozone depletion, and to get certain products off their shelves.

The project: Tell local store owners what ozone-depleting products they carry, and work to replace them.

THE OZONE-DESTROYERS

• Chlorofluorocarbons (CFCs) are among the most damaging ozone-depleters, and Americans are the world's heaviest CFC consumers. We use six times more CFCs than the global average.

• CFCs are most commonly used as coolants in refrigerators and air conditioners. But they're also in foam insulation, foam packaging, aerosol dust removers and other products. Many polystyrene foam products are made with modified CFCs, called HCFCs. These are less damaging...but they're still ozone-depleters.

• Methyl chloroform (also called 1,1,1, trichloroethane), used as a solvent, is weaker than CFCs, but is used in greater quantities. It's found in many home products, particularly in aerosol cans—even ones that say "ozone friendly" on the label.

• Halon—a potent ozone depleter—is used in fire extinguishers.

• Carbon tetrachloride (also called TCA) is a poisonous, nonflammable, colorless liquid typically used by chemical companies to make other chemicals.

• Freon is a CFC. It's often labeled on packages as R-1, or R-2. It's sold in cans at auto supply stores.

CFCs can take 8-12 years to reach the ozone layer.

WHAT YOU CAN DO

Before You Start

• Find out about the ozone layer. The guides listed here are excellent sources.

• Ozone depleters have several aliases; try to learn them all.

Shop Till They Drop

• Make a list of ozone-damaging products and take it shopping. Pick stores where you often shop. As a regular customer, your opinion carries weight. Grocery, hardware, auto supply and stereo stores all sell products that contain ozone-depleting compounds.

• Compare your list to the products the store carries.

• Share the list of ozone-depleting products with the store manager. Suggest alternatives. For example, aerosol dust removers that contain CFCs can be replaced with canned, compressed air. It works just as well for cleaning home stereo and photography equipment.

Letter Rip

• Check the labels; get manufacturers' names and addresses. Let them know you won't buy their products again until they're really "ozone friendly."

FOR FURTHER INFORMATION

• **Public Enemy 1,1,1..** The Natural Resources Defense Council, 1350 New York Ave., N.W. Washington, DC 20005. *A publication describing ozone-depleting products. NRDC also has information on ozone depletion and other environmental issues.* $15.95.

• **Background information and fact sheets on ozone-depleting compounds and products.** Local Solutions to Global Pollution, 2121 Bonar St., Berkeley, CA 94702. $5.

• **Protecting the Ozone Layer: What You Can Do.** Environmental Defense Fund, 257 Park Ave. South, New York, NY 10010. A citizen's guide to reducing the use of ozone-depleting chemicals.

See Also: "Hit The Road, Drac."

The refrigerators Americans buy in a week would make a tower more than 80 miles high.

29. ORGANIC MATTERS

It's estimated that 1 million people now suffer accidental
"severe acute" pesticide poisoning every year.

B ACKGROUND. Have you ever looked for organic produce
at your local grocery store? It's tough to find in many parts of
the U.S...which is hard to understand, since concern about
pesticides is growing rapidly.

If you want to buy organic food in your community, you have to
let your grocer know it. Use your power as a consumer to create
change.

DID YOU KNOW.

• The Natural and Organic Foods industry is now a $3 billion in-
dustry in the U.S., and organic purchases increased 68% in 1989.

• According to the California Certified Organic Farmers Association, supermarkets call requesting organic produce after the stores
receive as few as five letters from customers.

• In 1991, there were 84,000 conventional farmers in California
...and only 1,200 organic farmers. But the number of organic farmers is still four times as higher than it was in 1988.

WHAT YOU CAN DO

• Unless your state has a program requiring farmers to meet certain
standards, anyone can claim their food is organic or pesticide-free.
Find out about local regulations for organic produce. Ask a librarian to help, or write the National Coalition for Alternatives to Pesticides.

• See if any markets in surrounding areas carry organic produce. If
so, find out how they set it up. What you find out will help per-
suade your store manager that it can work.

Only one out of every four U.S. landfills monitors groundwater.

Wage a Campaign.

• Pick a store, and tell the manager and/or produce buyer you'd like them to stock organic produce. Save your receipts, then show the store owner how much produce you buy.

• Another approach: Write a letter. The store probably rarely gets letters, so even one will be noticed. Get other customers to sign it; store officials pay closer attention if they know others feel the way you do.

• If you're willing to pay a little more for pesticide-free produce, say so. But according to one consumer expert, "It costs the same for farmers to produce organic or non-organic produce—without chemicals, you can afford more labor."

• There's a good chance the manager will be responsive—consumer interest in the environment is increasing, and trying to accomodate your request is good public relations. It's also a good promotional opportunity for the store.

• Help find distributors. The store manager might not know where to find pesticide-free produce. Show him or her this "Resources" section.

RESOURCES

• **Pesticide Alert: A Guide to Pesticides in Fruits and Vegetables**, by Lawrie Mott and Karen Snyder. (Sierra Club, 1990). *An excellent guide that discusses the pesticides in America's produce.*

• **Diet For A Poisoned Planet,** by David Steinman. (Harmony Books, 1990). *This book discusses pesticides in our food, even pre-packaged items like milk and cookies.*

• **"What Organic Means,"** California Certified Organic Farmers, PO Box 8136, Santa Cruz, CA 95061. *Send SASE for free brochure.*

• **Pesticide Organizing Kit.** National Toxics Campaign Fund, 1168 Commonwealth Ave., Boston, MA 02134. $10.

• **Healthy Harvest III 1989-90**, Potomac Valley Press, 1424 16th St. NW, Washington, DC 20036. $18.25. *Includes lists of organic growers' associations around the country.*

95% of U.S. landfills have no way to collect toxic leachate if they detect it.

30. JOIN THE "INFANTRY"

As we've said before: Americans use 18 billion disposable diapers every year—enough to stretch to the moon and back 7 times.

BACKGROUND. We think cloth diapers are much better for the earth than disposables. Apparently a lot of people do, because the use of diaper services—which make cloth diapers easy to use—is growing.

Unfortunately, not every community has a diaper service yet. Maybe it's time for you to join the "infantry." Become a diaper activist. Bring a diaper service to your area.

MAKE MINE CLOTH

• The National Association of Diaper Services has 140 members; 40 of them—26% of the group— joined in 1990.

• Until recently, a study commissioned by Proctor & Gamble, the largest disposable diaper manufacturer, was the only source for comparisons between disposables and cloth diapers. You may have read, for example, that cloth diapers use more energy and more water than disposables—making the choice a toss-up.

• But a new study (Jan. 91) refutes those assertions. Its findings: manufacturing disposable diapers requires 6 times more energy than making cloth diapers.

• Disposable diapers generate seven times more waste than cloth—even taking into account that eventually cloth diapers will enter the waste stream.

WHAT YOU CAN DO

• Find out if there's a diaper service that will serve your neighborhood. Check the Yellow Pages. If there are none listed, call the National Association of Diaper Services (NADS). They'll tell you the nearest one. Call and ask if they deliver diapers to your area.

100,000 marine mammals die each year from eating or becoming entangled in plastic debris.

- **Many diaper services have a "moms-per-mile" policy**—they'll drive between 3 and 5 miles out of their boundary for each new customer. So even if you live 15 miles away from the nearest service area, you may only need to find 2 other parents near you who want to use a diaper service. Call them and see what it'll take to get them to expand to your area.

- **Look for other families that want diaper service.** Some ideas: Talk to parents at your nearby daycare center, in the PTA, in your childbirth class, or at your doctor's office.

- **Write a letter to the diaper service.** Tell them how many families would use the service. Get the families to sign the letter and have them include their addresses.

- **If the diaper service is a chain:** Send a copy to the corporate headquarters. They may also urge the local service to expand.

- **Follow it up. Stay in touch with the diaper service.**

- **If you find more than one diaper service nearby:** Write letters to all of them. Who knows—they may even compete to serve you.

A STEP FURTHER

- **Get your hospital to switch to a diaper service.** Chances are your hospital still uses disposables. An average-sized hospital delivers 500 babies and uses more than 5,000 diapers every year. If only 5% of American hospitals switched to cloth diapers, we'd keep more than 1.7 million diapers out of the waste stream.

FOR MORE INFORMATION

- **The National Association of Diaper Services.** 2017 Walnut St., Philadelphia, PA 19103. (800) 462-6237. *They can help you locate the diaper service nearest you.*

- **The King County Nurses Association.** 8511 15th Ave. N.E., Seattle, WA 98115. *They convinced the King's County Hospital to switch to cloth diapers. Send a SASE to get their diapering alternatives brochure.*

- **Diapers: Environmental Impacts and Life Cycle Analysis,** by Carl Lehrburger, Ph.D. P.O. Box 998, Great Barrington, MA 01230. *The study cloth diaper advocates have been waiting for—$40 for the complete report.*

As many as 38% of imported blackberries are contaminated with pesticides banned in the U.S.

31. START A DEMONSTRATION

Americans throw away 28 million tons of mowed grass, dead leaves, and branches every year—and all of it could be composted.

What do you do when you're finished raking the leaves? If you put them in a garbage bag and send them to a landfill, you're adding to the garbage crisis and wasting a resource that could make your soil richer.

The solution is home composting. . .but not everyone knows how to do it.

In more than 25 communities around the U.S., local governments are demonstrating the how-to's of backyard composting to interested citizens. This is a great way to spread the word. If you believe in composting, get a demonstration program started where you live.

DID YOU KNOW

• Composting yard waste is cleaner and healthier than burning it. Battelle Labs in Columbus, Ohio, estimates that every ton of leaves burned gives off 117 lbs of carbon monoxide, 41 lbs. of particulates, and seven or more carcinogens.

• Yard waste makes up about 20% of all the garbage Americans throw away. Composting these materials instead of dumping will help local landfills last longer…so fewer sites will have to be turned into garbage dumps.

• In Seattle, Washington, the city government teaches backyard composting techniques at neighborhood and community group meetings. The city also sells compost bins at cost to make it easy for people to compost in their backyards.

• Alameda County, California, has a mobile backyard composting display, including bins and handouts, which the county takes to parks and garden centers to teach backyard composting.

Every gram of compost contains a billion organisms.

WHAT YOU CAN DO

• **Get materials** about backyard composting and how to put on home composting education programs.

• **Find a sponsor for the project.** It can be your city or county government, an environmental or nature center, botanical garden or park department. If your city is typical, landfill space is getting scarcer and they have a garbage crisis on their hands—so it's in their interest to set up this kind of program.

• **Find a location.** Any outdoor public place where a display can be set up will do.

• **Get some handouts, brochures or leaflets.** You'll need educational materials that explain backyard composting, step-by-step, for people who visit the display.

• **It's important to have bins available** so people who come to the display can go right home and start composting. Bins, or kits to make bins, can be sold...or if there's funding available, they can be given away.

• **If there's no good permanent location**, set up a mobile display. The city can take the display to different locations, offering afternoon backyard composting workshops, handing out materials and selling bins.

RESOURCES

• An excellent summary of different ways to compost can be found in Robert Kourik's article in *Garbage* magazine, Nov./Dec. 1989, pp. 43-51.

• *"Making and Using Compost" Fact Sheet.* U.S. Dept. of Agriculture, Office of Communication, Washington DC 20250.

• **Make Compost in Fourteen Days.** Organic Gardening magazine, 33 East Minor St., Emmaus, PA 18098. A 60-page booklet for composting beginners. $3.

Americans throw away over 870,000 pounds of food a day.

FOR THE

COMMUNITY

32. AUDIT CITY HALL

*In 1988, Chicago taxpayers paid $38 million
just for the city government's electricity bills.*

BACKGROUND. You can't fight City Hall? Maybe not, but you can audit them. If you really want to make your local government environmentally aware, check to see that they're recycling, conserving energy and water, and carpooling. That's called an "environmental audit."

THE POWER OF CITY HALL

• People pay attention to elected officials. They can inspire a whole community to focus on conservation and work for the environment.

• Since the city government maintains roads, operates fire and police departments, and supports a maintenance crew, it can have an enormous direct impact on local environmental quality.

• City Hall can serve as a community "laboratory." If your local government selects and evaluates "green" products and services for its own use, it can help you decide which energy and resource saving items make the most sense for you.

BEFORE YOU START

• Put together a list of questions to ask. There's a sample list at the end of this section. But keep your own community in mind.

• Call your city councilmember, the city administrator, or the city manager. Tell them what you're doing and ask them to direct you to the city staff people who can answer your questions.

THE AUDIT

• Call or meet with city staff. Talk to maintenance staff about heating, the purchasing office about whether the city buys energy-efficient light bulbs, etc.

• Organize the information you gather. Use it to suggest changes.

The world's known oil reserves will last about 35 years at the rate we're using them.

• Give copies of your recommendations to each of the people you spoke with, the mayor and the members of the city council.

• Mail copies to the local paper, as well as civic and environmental organizations that might be interested.

SAMPLE QUESTIONS

Recycling

• Is there a system for office paper recycling in all city offices and buildings?
• Are there recycling facilities for glass and aluminum (e.g. in the the cafeteria and near vending machines)?
• Are there bins for recycling newspaper?
• Are city documents printed on both sides to save paper?

Coffee cups

• Do they use disposable cups or reusable mugs?

Water use

• Are there low-flow fixtures on city sinks and showers?
• Are water-saving toilet dams installed in city restrooms?
• Are drip systems and other conservation devices used on land-scaping?

Heating

• Are thermostats set at 68° F or lower?
• Are city buildings heated all the time, or is the heat turned off on nights and weekends?

Lighting

• Are lights in city buildings turned off nights and weekends?
• Does the city use energy saving light bulbs?

City Vehicles

• Does the city buy fuel-efficient cars for its fleet (and the police)?
• Are city vehicles tuned up regularly to ensure good mileage?

RESOURCE

• **50 Simple Things Your Business Can Do To Save The Earth, by the EarthWorks Group, $6.95** *Since city offices are like any other offices, this book will help with both the audit and your recommendations.*

There are over 1,500 curbside recycling programs in the U.S.

33. STREAM CONSCIOUSNESS

Federal and state agencies monitor the quality of only 30% of the surface water in the United States.

BACKGROUND. In 1986 students at Westwood Elementary School near Casper, Wyoming, adopted nearby Bolton Creek. Since then, they've planted more than 450 trees and shrubs along its banks to fight erosion.

In Virginia, volunteers organized by a chapter of Trout Unlimited removed more than 6 tons of trash and debris from the banks of the Four Mile Run stream.

Those are just a few examples of the way people are adopting their local streams and creeks. These vital parts of the eco-system are in trouble; they need our help.

Do you know any orphan streams? Wade right in.

STREAM SYMPTOMS

How healthy is your adopted stream? Its color and smell can tell you a lot.

• **Green water:** Can mean too much algae is in the water. It makes it hard for any other life to exist in the stream.

• **Muddy water:** Too much dirt in the water makes it hard for fish to breathe. The stream may need more plants along its bank to prevent erosion.

• **A shiny film on the water:** Can mean there's oil leaking into the stream.

• **Foam or suds in the water:** Can mean soap from homes or factories is leaking in.

• **Rotten egg smell:** Sewage could be leaking into the stream.

• **Orange or red coating on the water:** Could mean a factory is dumping pollutants into the stream.

Nearly 82% of all disposable diapers end up in landfills.

WHAT YOU CAN DO

See if anyone's already adopted a stream in your area. Check with local nature centers, park departments, garden clubs, service organizations or local environmental groups. If they have, join them. If not, find a community organization interested in supporting the effort. The Resources below will supply hints on how to work with the community to set up an adopt-a-stream program.

A GENERAL APPROACH

• **Investigate.** Find out what's been done to your stream, and what the town has planned for it. Learn its history, so you can restore it. Did it once have fish? What kinds of wildlife use it?

• **Decide on a program. You can:**

　♦ Pick up litter and debris along the stream and its banks.

　♦ Plant native plants along eroded parts of the bank.

　♦ Restock it with fish. (You can actually raise them in an aquarium and release them into the creek.) Check with your state Department of Fisheries or call a community college biology department for more information.

　♦ Set up a "pollution patrol," to report any signs of pollution. Groups like the Izaac Walton League can send you kits that help you monitor the water quality in your stream, and they can tell you who to report pollution to in your state.

　♦ Work with your town to keep the stream from being developed.

RESOURCES

• **The Adopt A Stream Foundation.** Box 5558, Everett, WA 98206. *One year membership, $25.00. Order their book "Adopting A Stream: A Northwest Handbook" for $9.95 plus postage.*

• **Save Our Streams Adoption Kit.** The Izaac Walton League of America, 1401 Wilson Blvd., Level B., Arlington, VA 22209. (703) 528-1818. $6.00. *Information on organizing a project, recognizing pollution, and restoring your stream. Send a SASE for more info.*

• **Trout Unlimited.** 800 Follon Lane, Suite 250, Vienna, VA 22180. (703) 281-1100. *National organization restoring trout, salmon, steelhead, and other fish with stream cleanups, etc.*

Newspapers are the single largest component of solid waste in landfills.

34. CURB YOUR RECYCLABLES

According to Biocycle, 400 communities started curbside recycling programs in 1989. Now over 1,000 communities have them.

BACKGROUND. Studies have shown that if you make it easy, people will recycle....And curbside recycling is as easy as it gets. With landfills overflowing, and natural resources more precious than ever, now is the time to get a curbside program started in your area.

DID YOU KNOW
• Each year Americans produce an average of over a half ton of garbage per person...and that figure is still growing.
• Every day Americans buy about 62 million newspapers...and throw away around 44 million of them. That's the equivalent of dumping 500,000 trees into landfills each week.
• In Seattle, Washington, 83% of homeowners participate in curbside recycling. In the first year of the program, the amount of garbage taken to Seattle landfills decreased by 22%.

WHAT YOU CAN DO
• Check to see if any towns near you have started a curbside recycling program. Find out how they did it.
• Figure out who's going to collect materials. See if the local garbage collection company would be willing to add curbside recycling to its services.
• In some places, community organizations run the curbside program and use the money they make to fund community programs.

Get Your City to Help
• Diana Gale, director of the Seattle Solid Waste Utility, encourages citizens to approach city governments about curbside pickup.

414 tons of dirty disposable diapers were discarded every hour in 1988.

"Politicians are very sensitive to recycling issues right now," she says. "They'll put recycling programs in because it's the right thing to do."

• The bottom line: Even if a curbside recycling program doesn't make a profit, it will save plenty on garbage collection and disposal costs. As the city manager of San Jose, California says, "It's cheaper to recycle a ton of waste than it is to collect it, haul it and dispose of it at a landfill."

• Note: The easiest way for people to remember when to put out their recyclables is to have curbside collection on the same day as garbage pick up.

• Any container can be used to hold recyclables—even old grocery bags and boxes. If your city sponsors the program, have them provide recycling bins.

• If you run into difficulties getting citywide curbside collection going, start a pilot program. Run a mini-curbside collection in a neighborhood to show people that it works. When people get used to it, they won't want to give it up.

• Publicize your project. Contact local news media, of course—but don't forget church newsletters, bulletin boards, handouts in grocery bags, etc.

RESOURCES
• **Why Waste A Second Chance: A Small Town Guide To Recycling,** National Association of Towns and Townships, 1522 K St., NW, Washington, DC, 20005. (202) 737-5200.

• **Waste To Wealth: A Business Guide For Community Recycling Enterprises,** Institute For Local Self-Reliance, 2425 18th St. NW, Washington, DC, 20009. (202) 232-4108. *A how-to guide for community groups and small businesses interested in establishing recycling programs. $37 postpaid.*

• **The Recycler's Handbook,** by the EarthWorks Group. Published by EarthWorks Press, 1400 Shattuck Ave, #25, Berkeley, CA 94709. *$5.95 postpaid, or look in local bookstores. A comprehensive guide to recycling for the beginner.*

Burning polystyrene foam produces 57 different chemical compounds, many of which are toxic.

35. MAKE YOUR CITY "BICYCLE-FRIENDLY"

The number of people cycling to work in the
U.S. has doubled in the past five years.

BACKGROUND. Bicycles are one of the most practical forms of alternative transportation. But they won't be used if it's not safe to ride them. Why not help give bicycles a piece of the road in your community?

DID YOU KNOW

• The most damaging auto pollution occurs in the first few minutes a car is running, when the engine is cold. So taking your bike on short trips instead of your car can eliminate substantial pollution.

• 50% of all commuting trips in the United States are less than 5 miles long. That only takes about 30 minutes by bicycle—less time if you're in good shape.

• In Sweden, office buildings are now being constructed with showers, so employees can ride their bikes to work.

WHAT YOU CAN DO

• **Contact bicycle organizations in your community.** Local clubs may already be working on bicycling issues; you can join them. Bicycle stores may know of clubs in your area.

• **Talk to people at city hall.** Ask for help in making the city bicycle friendly. Try the transportation planner, the traffic engineer, or the police department. Meet with your city council member.

• **Get support from community groups.** City governments will act when they see community support behind your project. So in addition to bicycle clubs, look for support from school groups, scout troops, etc. It's in everyone's interest to improve bicycling conditions.

• **Find out if there are bike lanes,** and if so, where they are. Are they on just one street, or is there a network throughout the city? If not, this is the place to start. If they are, work with the city or

As many as 75% of imported pineapples are contaminated with pesticides banned in the U.S.

bicycle clubs to print maps of them. They can be distributed at the public library, in schools, recreational centers, and in bike stores.

• **Push safety education programs** for bicyclists and motorists. Schools that teach bicycle safety, and driver education programs are important to protect cyclists and encourage bicycle use.

• **Lobby for adequate bicycle parking.** Bike parking areas and bicycle racks provide a convenient place to lock your bicycle. Some office building even have "bike rooms" where employees who commute by bicycle can park.

RESOURCES

• **Pro Bike Directory,** Bicycle Federation of America, 1818 R Street NW, Washington DC 20009. *Contains program information for individuals, organizations and government agencies on a local and national level.$15. This national Clearinghouse also has fact sheets and info on how to get more active on a local level. Send a SASE.*

• **Bicycle USA Almanac.** League of American Wheelmen, 6707 Whitestone Rd., Suite 209, Baltimore, MD 21207. (301) 944-3399. *A nationwide list of bicycling organizations, etc. You can get this and 8 copies of Bicycle USA as a member. $25/year membership.*

• **"Bicycle Legislation in U.S. Cities"** Local Solutions to Global Pollution. 2121 Bonar St. Studio A, Berkeley, CA 94702. *A packet of various cities' bicycle programs and policies. $7.00.*

There are at least 40 certified Farmer's Markets in Southern California.

36. SELL IT BY THE YARD

"Garage sales are a uniquely American sport."
—Dr. Douglas Ottati

BACKGROUND. Having a yard or garage sale is a good way to recycle *your* old things. But why think small? What if dozens—even hundreds—of households in your community held garage sales on the same day? In El Cerrito, California they did just that. It was a huge success—the local government and media got behind it and crowds of people showed up. It was a recycling bonanza.

IT'S GOOD FOR THE COMMUNITY

• It encourages reuse as a form of recycling by making it "official." People who might otherwise throw their old things out will participate if they see friends and neighbors getting involved.

• Promoting reuse in your community will ease the garbage crunch. At current dumping rates, more than 75% of our landfills will fill to capacity—and close—within 20 years.

• It sets an example. You'll spread the word to other communities that there are creative alternatives to dumping.

ORGANIZE!

• Approach your city government and get support for the project as a waste reduction or recycling event. Remind them that it will save landfill space and money. See if there's some incentive they can offer to help get people interested. In El Cerrito, the city government offered free earthquake inspections to participants.

• Recruit volunteers to work on the project.

• Set a date for the sale.

• Put together a registration form for people who want to participate, so they can tell you where they'll be holding their garage sales. (They fill in their names and addresses.) Then you

90% of the people who don't have mandatory recycling say they would support it.

use these completed forms to create a "shopper's map" or shopper's guide for the day of the event.

SPREAD THE WORD

• With city government involved, publicity shouldn't be a problem. They have contacts with the news media, and understand how to use them. They can distribute the maps.

• However, there's plenty your committee can do: Make flyers and signs to post in public places and key intersections (include maps) , get notices printed in community newsletters, put notices on bulletin boards, etc.

• See if you can get a local newspaper or radio station to "adopt" the event and give it an extra push.

• Make arrangements in advance for a charity organization to pick up the items that are left at the end of the day. Some charities will have a truck to go from house to house to pick them up, or you can arrange to drop them off.

Note: Garage sales are illegal in some communities; they're considered a nuisance instead of an opportunity to save resources and landfill space. If your town is one of them, lobby for a change.

RESOURCE

• **Garage Sale Mania,** Betterway Publications, PO Box 219, Crozet, VA 22932 (804) 823-5661 $10.00. *A rather strange book about holding and shopping at garage sales. It's the only one we know of.*

37. SHELLFISH PLEASURES

14 billion pounds of garbage are dumped in the world's oceans every year—most of it in the Northern Hemisphere.

BACKGROUND. Beach pollution is a growing problem. What can you do about it? Organize a community beach clean-up, or join the annual clean-up sponsored by the Center for Marine Conservation.

HIT THE BEACH

• In the 1989 National Beach Cleanup, volunteers in 25 states collected 3 million pieces of trash—nearly 900 tons of it.

• The types of trash collected during the clean-ups are recorded by CMC. It helps identify sources of pollution. For example, CMC traced more than 8,000 trash items to the petroleum industry in 1989. CMC can also use the evidence to expose violators of international anti-dumping treaties.

• In one clean-up, 8,000 plastic bags—which can injure marine animals that eat them—were found along 150 miles of North Carolina beaches.

WHAT YOU CAN DO

• **Pick a beach.** It doesn't have to be an ocean beach—it can be a wetlands area, a lakefront—even a large river bank.

• **Organize a group.** Contact local civic organizations, scout troops, and other service groups.

• **Set the date.** If possible, pick a day that coincides with other CMC-sponsored beach cleanups. The publicity generated by the national effort will help your project. And if you're part of CMC's effort, the information you gather will go into the national report on marine debris.

• **Get trash inventory forms.** CMC has forms that describe every imaginable type of trash. Use them to keep track of the items you

PET soda bottles are the most recycled plastic containers.

collect. Or make your own list.

- **Meet at the beach.** Divide up the beach so everybody has a segment. Give each person two bags—one for recyclable bottles and cans, one for everything else. Agree on a time to meet back at your central point.

- **Leave potentially hazardous items**—e.g., oil drums, containers of unidentified liquid, etc.—on the beach, but report them to authorities.

- **Separate and record trash at the end of the day.** This may not sound important, but it is. CMC's marine debris reports have influenced state, national and international ocean pollution policies.

- **Pack it out.** Recycle the bottles and cans. Take the rest to a landfill or other place where it can be disposed of properly.

A STEP FURTHER

Recycle Fishing Line

- Used fishing line strewn on piers and beaches is more than just a nuisance—it kills wildlife. On the day of CMC's 1989 beach cleanup, volunteers found 25 birds caught in fishing line.

- Berkley, a large fishing line manufacturer, accepts used nylon line and recycles it into useful products. Berkley provides dropoff bins free of charge to tackle stores. Check to see if your local store has one. If not, suggest they get one.

- No luck? You can send Berkley your fishing line through the mail: Berkley Recycling Center, P.O. Box 456 , Spirit Lake, IA 51360.

- Get a fishing line recycling bin set up at your local beach or pier. Find out who runs the beach or pier—the city, park district, state, etc. Let them know about Berkley's program.

RESOURCE

- **Center for Marine Conservation,** 1725 De Sales St., NW, Suite 500, Washington, DC 20036. (202) 429-5609. *They'll send you a free book called "All About Beach Cleanups" and other facts that will tell you what you need to organize a beach cleanup in your area.*

World population increased by 96 million in 1990.

38. YULE RECYCLE

Every year, Americans cut down an estimated 34 million Christmas trees—enough to cover the state of Rhode Island with a forest.

BACKGROUND. When the holiday season is over, what happens to your Christmas tree? Most trees end up in landfills. But they don't have to. Many communities have successful Christmas tree "recycling" programs. They collect trees and turn them into mulch, which is then used for gardening. If there isn't one in your community yet, why not help set one up?

DID YOU KNOW

• The first Christmas tree recycling programs were founded in 1971, in San Diego, California.

• Over 100 U.S. communities currently recycle Christmas trees.

• In Austin, Texas, the program is so successful that they now save more than $20,000 in hauling and disposal costs annually.

WHAT YOU CAN DO

• **Long before Christmas, call City Hall.** Ask them to sponsor it.

• **Will it be a curbside collection or a drop-off?** They can either have residents place trees on the curb for pick up, or set up a one- or two-day drop-off location.

• **They need a "chipper" or grinder.** That shouldn't be hard. Most cities and park districts have chippers they use to grind up tree trimmings and other vegetation into mulch.

• **They'll need to distribute the mulch.** The city should be prepared to coordinate the program with their parks and landscape maintenance crews. Remind them that it retards weed growth.

• **Advertise the program.** Christmas tree lots in your community can hand out flyers telling customers about the program and how to participate; the city's garbage collection service can put notices on people's trash cans telling them when to put their trees on the curb for collection; your local newspaper, radio stations and other media can feature articles and announcements on the program.

39. BE A GOVERNMENT AGENT

*In 1988, there were 20,350 violations of the Safe
Drinking Water Act in the state of New Jersey alone.*

BACKGROUND. Does your favorite pond smell like a chemical dump?
 Who do you report it to?
 Governments have limited resources to track pollution in our lakes, streams, and ponds. So they've begun getting people like us involved in monitoring and reporting it.

DID YOU KNOW

• Citizens can effectively call attention to pollution. For example, since 1983, more than 1,000 volunteers have monitored 85% of Massachusetts's lakes, streams and reservoirs.

• They found that more than half the state's water was being affected by acid rain. In response, the state passed laws to cut industrial emissions of sulfur dioxide—a chief cause of acid rain.

WHAT YOU CAN DO

Talk to regulators. Call the EPA, county health department, or whatever agency is in charge of monitoring water pollution in your area. Ask how you can help.

RESOURCES

• **"National Directory of Citizen Volunteer Environmental Monitoring Programs."** Rhode Island Sea Grant Information Office, URI Bay Campus, Marragansettri, RI 02882-1197. *Contains a lot of valuable details on monitoring programs, and lists more than 130 programs in 34 states, from Washington to Florida. Cost: $1.*

• **Volunteer Water Monitoring: A Guide for State Managers.** *Published by the EPA for regulators who work with citizens, it contains valuable background information.*

Employees at financial businesses generate about 2 lbs. of paper a day...per person.

40. PAINT THE TOWN

*The EPA has found more than 300 toxic substances
in commercial oil and latex paints.*

BACKGROUND. How much paint is stashed in your garage or basement? If you're an average American, you've got about four gallons of it. Did you know that it's considered a hazardous waste...and shouldn't be thrown in the garbage. So what can you do with it? Some communities have developed paint exchange programs—"drop & swaps" where people bring reusable paint to trade or give away. It's the most environmentally effective way to deal with old paint.

PIGMENTS OF IMAGINATION

• According to *Resource Recycling* magazine, Santa Monica, California, started one of the nation's first paint exchanges in late 1985. "Groups and individuals are welcome to take any paint they need among the usable paint brought into the city's permanent household hazardous waste (HHW) collection facility." They say it's estimated that 75% of the paint the city collects is taken at paint exchanges. They give away 25 to 75 gallons of paint each month—mostly to an artist's cooperative and a painting contractor.

• The magazine also reports that "paint exchanges work well in a number of Minnesota communities....Paint exchanges in Kandiyohi County and St. Cloud have resulted in 65-75% reductions in the amount of paint that must be landfilled."

WHAT YOU CAN DO

• Find out if there's already a paint exchange program in town. Ask the fire department or county government (counties are more likely to be the sponsors of HHW facilities).

• If there's no paint exchange, and no one seems willing to get one going, limit your efforts to your neighborhood.

NEIGHBORHOOD EXCHANGE

If you're interested in trading in your neighborhood, here are a few things you should know:

• Keep oil-based and latex paints separate.

• Check for paint hardening and spoilage. Shake cans to see if contents are still liquid; latex paint is spoiled if it's the consistency of curdled milk.

• Air-dry spoiled paint. Dispose of cans with hardened latex paint in your garbage. Be sure to save all hardened oil-based paints for a household hazardous waste collection. Call your hazardous waste office for details.

• Don't accept or reuse pre-1978 or non-residential paints. They may contain lead.

• The EPA has banned mercury from indoor paint because the fumes are harmful. Paint marked "exterior" or "indoor/outdoor" probably contains it. To check whether paint has mercury, call the National Pesticide Telecommunications Network, (800) 858-7378. To be safe, don't reuse pre-1991 paints containing any level of mercury (which is toxic)...or paint labeled for exterior or indoor-outdoor use. Clearly label any paints that are for exterior use only.

• Any other questions? Call the household hazardous waste office.

• **A word from Lois Epstein, of the Environmental Defense Fund:** "Use the paint swap to educate family and neighbors on environmentally sound paint use. Highlight the importance of not buying more paint than you need for a particular job, so wastes are minimized, of ventilating newly painted areas during and after painting, and minimizing the presence of children and pets in these areas...and of using latex paints rather than oil/solvent-based paints whenever possible....Never pour paints containing mercury into the sink, drain or toilet, since mercury that enters water systems can form methyl mercury, a highly toxic compound."

RESOURCES

• **Paint Drop & Swap: Guidelines for Conducting Events,** Vermont Agency of Natural Resources. $5 from Vermont Solid Waste Division, 103 S. Main St., West Building, Waterbury, VT 05676, Attn. Andrea Cohn.

The average baby generates a ton of garbage every year.

41. HIT THE ROAD, DRAC

Vehicle air conditioners are the single largest users of CFCs in the U.S.

BACKGROUND. Usually, when your air conditioner or refrigerator is serviced, the mechanic just lets the coolants—ozone-depleting CFCs—escape into the atmosphere. But they don't have to. There's a device called a "vampire" that can remove coolants from appliances and trap them in bottles for recycling. It's an important innovation, and every business that repairs refrigerators or car air conditioners should have one.

DID YOU KNOW
• According to the *Washington Post*, "Loss of ozone is worse than we thought. Atmospheric ozone has decreased by as much as 3% over densely populated areas of North America and Europe just since 1969."

• Refrigerators and car air conditioners are the #1 source of CFCs in the United States.

• The Natural Resources Defense Council estimates that car air conditioners alone may be responsible for 16% of ozone depletion.

WHAT YOU CAN DO

Get your local auto repair shop to buy and use a vampire unit.
• Contact the owner of the garage that services your car, or your refrigerator repairman. Ask if they use a vampire unit. If not, tell them about it.

• Point out the value of being able to advertise that their business is "ozone friendly."

Get Your City to Require CFC Recycling.
• If you'd like to get more involved with this issue, talk to your city council about passing a law requiring car air conditioner and refrigerator repair facilities to capture and recycle CFCs. Denver, Colo-

States with bottle deposit laws have 30-40% less litter by volume.

rado; Irvine, California; Independence, Oregon; and Newark, New Jersey, have all passed CFC recycling laws.

• **Push for a "Refrigerator Roundup."** When refrigerators and air conditioners are discarded, CFCs eventually escape into the atmosphere. One alternative: Get your city or local landfill operator to set up a CFC reclamation program for old refrigerators. The Nature Center in Kalamazoo, Michigan, has a refrigerator roundup program for their community. Contact them for information.

RESOURCES

• **Recovering and Recycling CFCs.** Local Solutions to Global Pollution, 2121 Bonar St., Studio A, Berkeley, CA 94702. *Includes a list of equipment, manufacturers, and CFC recycling facilities. $5.*

• **Local Government CFC Ordinances.** *Also available from Local Solutions to Global Pollution. Contains copies of CFC ordinances that cities have passed, $6.*

• **Joe Arguello,** 1339 Gay St., Longmont, CO 80501. (303) 678-9953. *He successfully started his own CFC recycling business.*

MORE OZONE ACTIVISTS

• **Protecting the Ozone Layer: What You Can Do.** Environmental Defense Fund, 257 Park Ave. South, New York, NY 10010. (212) 505-2100. A citizen's guide to reducing the use of ozone depleting chemicals. Call for prices and info.

• **Saving the Ozone Layer: A Citizen Action Guide.** Natural Resources Defense Council. 40 W. 20th St., New York, NY 10011.

• **Kalamazoo Nature Center,** 7000 N. Westnedge Ave., Kalamazoo, MI 49007. (616) 381-1574. *Call or send a SASE to get information on their Refrigerator Roundup program.*

Recycling half the world's paper would free 20 million acres of forestland.

42. COMMUNITY RE-LEAF

*A full grown birch tree provides enough
oxygen for a family of four people.*

Anybody can plant a tree, but it's easier—and more fun—when people do it together. With a little effort, you can branch out into your community and create a one-day tree-planting event.

DID YOU KNOW

• In many areas, we're chopping down trees faster than we're planting them. For example, Nebraska has lost 30% of its forestland in the past 10 years.

• Trees absorb carbon dioxide—the main greenhouse gas. One acre of trees can absorb as much as four tons a year.

• Trees save energy. Shade trees reduce air-conditioning needs by up to 50%. And in the summer, they can keep cities as much as 15% cooler.

• In addition to improving the surroundings, tree-planting has become a popular way for people to work together to help the environment For example, California Re-Leaf plans to plant 20 million trees by the year 2000. So far, they've planted over 300,000 of them.

WHAT YOU CAN DO
Take Care of the Basics

• Contact the American Forestry Association or TreePeople for info on picking and planting trees...and what you'll need to do it. Think about native trees; they'll probably require less care.

• Pick a site. It may be easiest to get permission to plant trees on public land.

On average, an acre of land contains more than 3 million earthworms.

• The nursery is an obvious place to get trees, but there may be other places. Check with nearby college agricultural departments, and U.S. forestry offices. City governments will often provide trees at cost.

• How many people will be involved? If it's a small project, ask friends and neighbors to help. If you want to involve more people, ask at local service organizations.

• Ask newspapers, TV, or radio stations to publicize your project with a "public service announcement."

Pick a date

• Arrange for volunteers to meet at the planting site with the tools they need. Don't forget about lunch—are you providing it, or are they? A pot-luck is a great idea.

• If possible, arrange to deliver trees on planting day—it's best to plant them fresh. Organize a crew to pick them up from the nursery. Or see if your nursery delivers.

• Keep an eye on your trees. Young trees need care. So organize a "tree maintenance team."

Use an "adopt a tree" program to help pay your expenses

• Once you've organized the project, ask people and/or businesses to sponsor trees for a fee that approximates the cost of planting and maintaining them.

RESOURCES

• **"Planting Trees."** Pennsylvania Resources Council, P.O. Box 88, Media, PA 19063. *Instruction pamphlet for tree planting. Send a SASE. Free for single copies or $16.00 for 100 copies.*

• **TreePeople,** 12601 Mulholland Dr., Beverly Hills, CA 90210. (818) 753-4600. *Call or Write for info, or send $12.95($13.79 in California) + $4.00 shipping and handling for their book: "The Simple Act of Planting a Tree."*

• **American Forestry Association,** Global Releaf Program, PO Box 2000, Washington, D.C. 20013. (202) 667-3300. *Their Global Releaf program has set a goal of planting 100 million trees by 1992. Write or call for information on their campaign.*

It has been reported that the average American can save 72 lbs. of glass in a year.

43. IT'S OIL
WE CAN DO

*U.S. car owners throw away more than 120 million
gallons of recoverable motor oil every year.*

BACKGROUND. After you change the oil in your car,
you've got about five or six quarts of toxic sludge to get rid
of. In *50 Simple Things You Can Do to Save the Earth*, we
talked about recycling it. But not every community has a place to
take it. Why not work to change more than your oil? Get a recycling center started.

DID YOU KNOW

• Motor oil never wears out—it only gets dirty. So there's no
reason to throw it away. Oil can be "re-refined," a process that removes the dirt so the oil can be used again.

• Recycled motor oil is identical to new oil. Nonetheless, we throw
away enough motor oil every year to fill 120 supertankers.

• Many communities in the U.S. don't have public oil collection
facilities. But a 1985 survey by the Department of Energy found
that 75% of home oil changers would recycle their oil *if* there was a
facility nearby.

WHAT YOU CAN DO

• See what oil recycling facilities are available in your area. Call
the EPA at (202) 382-7932 and find out who to contact in your
state, or ask at gas stations and auto repair shops.

• If you find there's already a facility, tell people about it—chances
are they don't know it exists.

To Set Up A Motor Oil Collection Facility

• In most communities, there are three places where it's practical
to set up used oil collection: at a gas station or auto repair garage, a
recycling center, or the maintenance garage of your local government.

Corporations spend millions to get 1% market shares—they listen to consumers.

- Your best bet: The local government's garage. They should be doing it themselves, and it's their responsibility to make sure you don't dump it somewhere else.

- In some states—California, for example—recycling centers are allowed to collect small quantities of motor oil without getting a special permit for storing hazardous materials.

- Gas stations used to accept do-it-yourselfers' motor oil routinely. But since it's been classified a hazardous waste, they've been reluctant to accept it (insurance issues are a primary reason). One reaction: some local governments are requiring anyone who sells motor oil to take used oil back for recycling or disposal in a hazardous waste dump. That's an incentive for recycling. According to some sources, it costs 10¢-20¢ a gallon to have used oil picked up for recycling; but it costs up to $4 to dispose of it at a hazardous waste collection site.

- What happens to the oil after it's collected? A trucker picks it up and takes it to a re-refiner. To find a trucker, check the Yellow Pages under "Oils—Waste."

If everyone turns you down, go public with it. Contact your local newspaper, ask for an assignment editor or local reporter, and suggest they write an article about it. Or call a TV or radio station.

- Another effective alternative: Write a letter to the editor of your local paper. With recycling—and hazardous waste—receiving so much attention, people are bound to take notice.

RESOURCES

- **"How to Set Up a Local Program to Recycle Used Oil"**, (EPA/530-89-039a) Environmental Protection Agency, Office of Solid Waste and Emergency Response, 401 M St. SW (OS-305), Washington, DC 20460, (800) 424-9346. *A manual for environmental groups, and community organizations. They also have free brochures on what to do with used oil.*

- **Project Rose**, PO Box 870203, Tuscaloosa, AL, 35487-0203 (205)348-4878. *They assist communities and citizens in setting up local oil recycling plans. Send a letter of inquiry with a SASE.*

Activist Tim McClure once staked a mining claim on a landfill to promote recycling.

44. HOWDY, NEIGHBOR

U.S. industries generate nearly 2 tons of toxic waste for every man, woman, and child in America annually.

BACKGROUND. Some environmentalists think of all businesses as adversaries. But that doesn't help anyone. In fact, many businesses—even ones that produce hazardous waste—are willing to modify practices in order to be better neighbors. That's the basis for a new kind of cooperation between industry and concerned citizens. It's called a "good neighbor agreement."

RIGHT NEIGHBORLY

• Good neighbor agreements put in writing what you and local industries believe is responsible corporate behavior.

• Good neighbor agreements increase a community's influence with local industries. A good neighbor agreement, backed up by on-site inspections, keeps you up to date on local industry activities.

• One example: The American Brass & Iron Foundry in Oakland, California, a major user of ozone-depleting chemicals, agreed to phase out all releases by 1997 in a good neighbor agreement signed with Citizens for a Better Environment and Greenpeace Action.

WHAT YOU CAN DO

Before You Start

• If you and your neighbors have a problem with a business in your neighborhood—excessive odor or noise from a factory, or leaky drums in storage, for instance—or if you're just concerned about potentially hazardous chemicals, call the company and ask to meet with the plant manager or other company representative.

• In your meeting, bring notes of what the problem is and when it has occurred. Be clear, thorough, and let them know you'd like to work with them to solve the problem.

Every year, the U.S. harvests as much grass from lawns as the Japanese harvest rice.

• Negotiate the good neighbor agreement. Work with the company to find an acceptable compromise. This doesn't mean you should give up on the points that mean the most to you— just be open to other points of view.

• Your agreement might include reduction of the use of a particularly toxic chemical, training for workers handling toxics, and improved notification when accidents occur.

• Remember—if you can, try to maintain a good working relationship with the people at the company.

If you aren't satisfied with their response.

• Call your city government or EPA.

• Most states have hazardous materials "disclosure laws," and many cities have "community right-to-know" laws. They require businesses to report the toxic and hazardous materials use or store on their premises.

• Call the National Toxics Campaign to find out which state agency you need to contact, or use the Toxic Release Inventory database. We show you how to use it on page 118.

RESOURCES

• **National Toxics Campaign: The Citizen's Toxics Prevention Manual.** 37 Temple Place, 4th Floor, Boston, MA 02111 (617) 482-1477. *Ask for a copy of their list of publications.*

• **Citizen's Clearinghouse for Hazardous Wastes.** P.O. Box 926, Arlington, VA 22216. (703) 276-7070. *They publish a hazardous waste fact book, a guide to using right-to-know laws, and a guide to investigating polluting companies. Call or write for a list of publications.*

• **Using Community Right-to-Know Laws.** The Center for Neighborhood Technology, 2125 West North Ave., Chicago, IL 60647. (312) 278-4800. *Call or write for a copy of this article.*

A recent survey found that 3 out of 4 people think anti-pollution laws are too weak.

45. GOOD BUY AGAIN

The state of Maryland has been buying recycled paper since 1977.

BACKGROUND. Picture the supply room of any government office. Stacks of computer paper, message pads, file cards...endless office supplies. Most of these products aren't made of recycled materials.

Government has a lot of purchasing power...and it should be used to support the recycling industry. So get your local government to change their buying policies and use recycled goods.

BUY IT AGAIN, SAM

• Every year, state and local governments buy nearly $80 billion worth of products—about 13% of the Gross National Product.

• If even a fraction of this was spent on recycled products, it would have a huge impact. One of the most common complaints about buying recycled goods is that: they cost more. But this is almost entirely due to the limited market. Government purchasing is the easiest way to expand that market.

• When local governments switch to recycled goods, suppliers have to meet the demand. The result: recycled goods become more affordable, giving everyone a chance to make the switch.

WHAT YOU CAN DO

Find Out What's Available

• What products currently used by your government could be replaced with recycled goods? Start with recycled paper—it's a fairly easy item to locate.

• If you want to go further, look into things like recycled building materials, "glasphalt" (asphalt made with recycled glass), retreaded tires and recycled oil for city vehicles.

• Get copies of policies that other towns have already enacted. It will give your government a head start. Newark, New Jersey; St. Paul, Minnesota; and Santa Cruz County and the city of San Jose, California have all adopted recycled products purchasing policies.

BUY THE WAY

• Call City Hall and find out who's in charge of purchasing. City Councils or town administrators usually make overall policy and purchasing managers implement it. If you have trouble getting the information, ask your city councilmember for help.

• Get details on the city's purchasing policy. Most local governments only require that products be bought from the company with the lowest price. Your town may intentionally exclude recycled materials from consideration, assuming that the quality is lower.

• Volunteer to help get the policy adopted. This might include collecting signatures on a petition or finding out about companies that sell or manufacture goods made of recycled materials.

• Keep an eye on the proposal. If any public hearings are held, get as many people as you can to attend the meeting and show support.

FOR FURTHER INFORMATION

• **The Government Procurement Kit,** $9. Conservatree Information Services, 10 Lombard St., Suite 250, San Francisco, CA 94111. (415) 453-1000. *Topics include: "Creating Markets For Recycling," and "Municipal Government Recycled Purchasing Policies." Call or write for their publications.*

• **The Greenline Newsletter.** *Also available from Conservatree. Their "Greenline" membership entitles you to six bimonthly issues and many other materials involving recycled paper. Send a SASE to get more information, or subscribe for $29.*

• **Local Government Procurement and Market Development.** $8.50. Local Government Commission, 909 12th St., Ste. 205, Sacramento, CA 95814. (916) 448-1198. *A how-to guide for local governments interested in adopting a recycled product purchasing policy.*

• **The Recycled Products Guide,** *a catalog of recycled products which is updated and published three times a year. Contains over 1,500 listings.* (800) 267-0707. *$195 a year; $105 for a single issue.*

In one $650,000 debt-for-nature swap, Bolivia agreed to protect 3 million acres of rainforest.

46. STOP SPRAYING

According to a recent Gallup poll, "73% of Americans think we should use fewer pesticides."

BACKGROUND. How does your local government control insect pests and weeds? Most likely, with heavy doses of chemicals.

Although many people don't realize it, there are effective, proven alternatives to pesticides and herbicides. It's time for you—and your local government—to look into them.

DID YOU KNOW

• Northwest Coalition for the Alternatives to Pesticides says that "Less than 10 of the roughly 600 commonly used pesticide 'active ingredients,' have been completely tested." Many are suspected carcinogens.

• According to Worldwatch Institute, "The federal government has set drinking water standards for only six pesticides—none of which are among the 17 that EPA reports have contaminated groundwater."

• One result: In 1986 Florida officials have had to close down 1,000 wells used for drinking water because of excessive levels of pesticides and other toxics.

• The most effective alternative to pesticides is called IPM, or "integrated pest management." In 1971, the city of Berkeley, California started an IPM program. Within the first year they reduced spending on pest control by 90%. The National Park Service also uses IPM.

WHAT YOU CAN DO

• **Here are some ideas:** Stop the use of pesticides in your nearby park; get your city to eliminate pesticides on street trees; or set up a neighborhood pesticide agreement (neighbors agree to eliminate spraying pesticides or to notify the neighborhood before spraying).

A 20' X 20' space in your backyard will support as many as 6 dwarf fruit trees.

- If you want to ban pesticides in your neighborhood, call your neighbors together. If your goal is to get a policy in your city or parks, to invite other people in the community who share your concerns. Set your goals and divide tasks.

- Work with the city staff member in charge of pest management activities. Call City Hall and find out who's in charge.

- Ask what kinds of pests are a problem in your city, and what pesticides the city's using to control them.

- When you know which pesticides are being used, check out the Resources section and track down alternatives. Being able to suggest specific alternatives to pesticide use will help demonstrate to the city that they don't have to spray.

- Present your information and ideas to your city council member: Ask if he or she would support adopting a "pesticide free" policy for city-owned property and get the city to use alternatives.

- **Note:** If you have trouble getting your city to agree to a no-pesticide policy, try getting them to at least agree to a "notification requirement." This requires that notices be posted in areas before they're sprayed.

SOURCES

- **Northwest Coalition for Alternatives to Pesticides (NCAP).** P.O. Box 1393, Eugene, OR 97440. (503) 344-5044. *A clearinghouse for alternatives to pesticides and publisher of the* Journal of Pesticide Reform. *Call or send a SASE for a list of publications.*

- **National Coalition Against the Misuse of Pesticides (NCAMP),** 701 E. St., SE, Washington, D.C., 20003. (202) 543-5450. *Good source of information on pesticide alternatives. They publish a newsletter called* Pesticides and You. *Send a SASE.*

- **Bio-Integral Resource Center (BIRC).** P.O. Box 7141, Berkeley, CA 94707. (415) 524-2567. *Publishers of Common Sense Pest Control Quarterly. Call or send a SASE for catalog.*

A pan of beer in your garden will help keep snails out.

47. TEACH AN OLD BUILDING NEW TRICKS

A water heater blanket can save up to 10% of the energy the heater uses.

BACKGROUND. Energy conservation is an important environmental concern, and one effective way to save energy in any community is passing "retrofit" laws. These laws require that buildings be inspected whenever they're sold or renovated, to see if they meet simple energy conservation measures. If not, the owner has to bring them up to minimum standards.

DID YOU KNOW

• Most states have energy conservation standards for new construction, but what about existing buildings? Requiring retrofitting of existing buildings is one of the most effective energy-saving steps a city government can take.

• The suggested measures include: replacing insulation that's not up to standard, weatherizing doors and windows, and putting blankets on hot water heaters.

• A number of local and state governments have already adopted energy conservation legislation. San Francisco's Residential Energy Conservation Ordinance (RECO), adopted in 1982, has saved more than $8 million in energy costs for local residents. Based on RECO's success, San Francisco adopted a commercial Energy Conservation Ordinance which is expected to save local businesses more than $40 million in its first five years.

• Energy conservation reduces utility bills, saving money for consumers. Conservation measures are far more cost effective than building new power plants.

WHAT YOU CAN DO
To Get a Retrofit Ordinance Passed:
• Learn what energy conservation measures are appropriate for old-

2.6 billion lbs. of pesticides are applied to American fruits and vegetables every year.

er buildings. If you want building owners and city officials to support a retrofit ordinance, it's a good idea to have information about the most cost-effective conservation measures available. Your local utility, the library and the organizations listed below are good sources of information. Put together a few concrete examples of how much energy can be saved—and how much utility bills will go down.

• **Drum Up Community Support.** When you're trying to get a law passed, it helps to be able to demonstrate that the community is solidly behind the idea. Talk to environmental organizations, the chamber of commerce or other business associations, your local utility company and other community groups.

• **Meet with your City Councilmember.** Talk to him or her about the benefits of retrofitting and point out the community support for the ordinance. Ask him or her to sponsor the law. Many cities may require a number of reviews before a new law can be passed. Find out what's required in *your* city and ask what you can do to help.

RESOURCES

•**"Model Ordinances for Environmental Protection,"** Local Government Commission, 909 12th St., Suite 205, Sacramento, CA 95814. *Includes a copy of San Francisco's ordinance for commercial buildings and a description of what retrofit ordinances do.* $10.

•**Public Utilities Commission,** Bureau of Energy Conservation, City and County of San Francisco, 110 McCallister St., Room 402, San Francisco, CA 94102. *Write for a brochure on commercial energy conservation. Free.*

Tomatoes need at least 6 hours of direct sunlight every day.

48. THE BEST IN THEIR FIELDS

The grand opening of The Southern Maryland Regional Farmer's Market attracted 10,000 people.

BACKGROUND. Farmer's markets are like street fairs. You get outside, walk around, see what everyone's up to. And there's the added bonus locally grown food.

Farmers appreciate it, too—they have a place to sell their goods for a reasonable price.

If there's no farmer's market in your community, maybe you should help organize one.

LETTUCE ENTERTAIN YOU

• The food on the average American dinner plate has traveled 1,300 miles to get there. So buying produce from local farmers saves fuel...and reduces pollution.

• One out of every $11 you spend on food goes for packaging. Buying fresh from farmers cuts down on trash.

• Farmers usually sell 90% of the produce they bring to farmer's markets.

• Most of the produce sold at farmer's markets is harvested no earlier than two days before you buy it. In a grocery store the product could have been harvested weeks before.

• In California, half of all organic farmers sell their produce at farmers markets.

WHAT YOU CAN TO

To Get Started:

• Call or write your state Department of Agriculture to get a list of farmer's markets in your area. Contact the people who run them for advice on setting up a market in your area.

• The support of an established organization is a big help in getting a farmer's market started. Local gardening clubs, environmental groups and service organizations like 4-H may be interested.

- There may be city, county, or even state regulations you need to know about. Contact your state Department of Agriculture and local health department for information.

- If you plan to sell more than produce (e.g. crafts or packaged foods), there may be special regulations to find out about.

- If your market needs city permits...or if you want to locate it on city land, it'll help to have a friendly contact in City Hall.

Plan It Out

- You'll need start-up funds for publicity, telephones, permit fees, recruiting farmers, and possibly insurance.

- Decide when the market will be open. Some markets are seasonal, some are open on weekends, etc.

- The best site is one that's visible, easy to get to, and free. It can be on public or private land. One idea: A local shopping center might let you use space in its parking lot. Other ideas: Downtown plazas or blocked-off streets.

Recruit local farmers

- Contact your state or county Department of Agriculture—they'll have names and numbers of organic farmer and small farmer associations in your area. They may even already have a list of farmers interested in selling at farmer's markets.

- A farmer's market is like any business—it takes a little time to get going. Get the farmers to agree in advance to participate for a couple of months, so the market has a chance to get established. One idea: Sell "season passes"— the farmers pay once, and can sell their goods for an entire month

- Publicize your market. Some suggestions: TV and radio public service announcements, articles in your local paper, signs at your location—even when it's closed. Keep it up, even after the market is established—and keep new customers coming.

RESOURCES

- **"Organizing a Certified Farmer's Market."** California Dept. of Food and Agriculture, Direct Marketing Program, 1220 N St., Rm. A-287, Sacramento, CA 95814. *Specifically tailored for California but has good general info for people who really want to start a market. It's free. Send a SASE.*

ne study has found that 63% of domestic and imported strawberries contain the pesticide Palert.

49. IT'S YOUR RIGHT TO KNOW

22.5 billion pounds of hazardous chemical releases were reported to the Toxic Release Inventory Database in 1987.

BACKGROUND. On December 4, 1984, a cloud of methyl isocyanate gas escaped from a Union Carbide Plant in Bhopal, India, killing 2,500 people and injuring tens of thousands more. In response to this tragedy, the U.S. Congress passed the Emergency Planning and Right-to-Know Act. It entitles you to know about the amounts, location, and potential effects of hazardous chemicals present in your community.

WHAT DOES THE LAW DO FOR YOU?

• This law established the toxic release data base, a nationwide resource which tracks the whereabouts and use of about 320 toxic chemicals.

• The data base is available in at least one library in every county in the United States, for public use—either on microfilm or in a computer. So if you want to know what toxic emissions are being released in your community, call your library.

• 20,000 industrial plants across the nation are reporting their toxic emissions under the auspices of this law.

RESOURCES

• **The EPA Community Right to Know Hotline (800) 535-0202** *Open 8:30 am to 7:30 pm EST. They can send you detailed fact sheets about most of the chemicals you find in the TRI database.*

• **Working Group On Community Right-to-Know,** 215 Pennsylvania Ave, SE, Washington, DC 20003,(202) 546-9707. *The monthly newsletter,"Working Notes on Community Right-to-Know," is a working paper on toxics that chronicles what's going on. $15/year. Also ask for introductory packet and a full list of 16 resource packets.Send a SASE.*

250,000 Californians get their electricity from a solar power plant in the Mojave Desert.

50. CREATE YOUR OWN PROJECT

You may have expected more "simple things" when you first picked up this book. But if you've gotten this far, you know that simple things are only one part of environmental activism. Sometimes, creating change takes more effort.

Hopefully, a project or two in this book inspired you to get out and do something in your community—plant a garden, help make the streets safe for bicyclists, add environmental education to your PTA's agenda...or any of the other 50 More Things.

But what really matters is that you realize you have the power to make these projects happen. The more responsibility you're willing to take on...the more people you can inspire...the more enthusiastic you become...the greater the impact you'll have on our planet.

Our 50 things are just suggestions. We're sure you have your own ideas...and want to hear about your successes. Write to us.

THE EARTHWORKS GROUP
1400 Shattuck Avenue, #25
Berkeley, California 94703

Gaps around windows and doors of an average house can equal a hole in the wall 3' x 3'.

Don't Forget:
You Can Make
a Difference.